PRAISE FOR *TINY EXPERIMENTS*

"I loved this profound, practical, and generous book. Through the ingenious lens of the tiny experiment, Anne-Laure Le Cunff shows how we can jettison arduous and dispiriting attempts at self-improvement in favor of achievable and energizing adventures on the path to a more vibrant, accomplished, and wholehearted life."

—Oliver Burkeman, *New York Times* bestselling author
of *Four Thousand Weeks*

"The fear of failure often stands in the way of learning from trial and error. This is a thought-provoking guide to doing more trials and making fewer errors."

—Adam Grant, #1 *New York Times* bestselling author of *Think Again* and
Hidden Potential and host of the podcast *Re:Thinking*

"Anne-Laure Le Cunff shows how to separate ambition from rigid linear goals, allowing uncertainty to bloom into possibility and a meaningful life to emerge organically. A compelling new take on a timeless concern."

—Cal Newport, *New York Times* bestselling author
of *Slow Productivity* and *Deep Work*

"*Tiny Experiments* is a breath of fresh air in a world that loves to complicate things. This book is the nudge we all need to live a more playful, experimental life—and isn't that what we're really here for?"

—Tara Schuster, author of *Buy Yourself the F*cking Lilies*

"Clear, practical, inspiring. This book will change the way you design your goals and live your life."

—Nir Eyal, bestselling author of *Indistractable*

"One of those books that changes the way you think, over and over again, for the better. This is easily one of the best productivity books that I've read: a rigorously researched, deeply delightful, and powerfully practical solution for turning our work into play."

—Ryder Carroll, creator of the Bullet Journal and *New York Times* bestselling
author of *The Bullet Journal Method*

"A must read for anyone who struggles with uncertainty (most of us humans!). This intelligent and actionable book offers new tools for how to learn from and even collaborate with uncertainty."

—Liz Fosslien and Mollie West Duffy, bestselling coauthors of *No Hard Feelings*

"A science-backed toolkit for embracing uncertainty as a catalyst for growth rather than a source of anxiety. This book is your permission slip to live life on your own terms, guided by curiosity and meaningful exploration."

—Melody Wilding, LMSW, author of *Trust Yourself*

"Whether you're looking to improve your health, career, or creativity, *Tiny Experiments* is a powerful guide to embracing curiosity and developing an experimental mindset. Perfect for anyone seeking more freedom in how they design their life."

—Ali Abdaal, *New York Times* bestselling author of *Feel-Good Productivity*

"A paradigm-shifting exploration of how to apply the techniques of science to the often crazy, chaotic, and highly uncertain domain of navigating your career and life in the modern world. An actionable toolkit for crafting a life so unique that it could only belong to you."

—Tiago Forte, *Wall Street Journal* bestselling author of *Building a Second Brain*

"The urge to start experimenting will hit you around page two, and it just builds from there. *Tiny Experiments* is an inspiring, tangible playbook to break past the status quo of our overwhelmed generation."

—Jo Franco, creator of JoClub and author of *Fluentish*

"A compelling case for an experimental mindset, this book is a call to action for anyone ready to explore life through the lens of curiosity."

—Ana Lorena Fábrega, author of *The Learning Game*

"An essential handbook for our modern era—an era defined not by linear definitions of success, but by the squiggles and swerves necessary to thrive in a rapidly changing world. *Tiny Experiments* will fundamentally alter how you think about and live your life."

—Simone Stolzoff, author of *The Good Enough Job*

"One of the first books I've read that goes far beyond critiquing the flaws with the modern default path of work, daring us to imagine a more expansive form of ambition: one built not on what might impress others, but on what will make a life worth living."

—Paul Millerd, author of *The Pathless Path* and *Good Work*

TINY EXPERIMENTS

TINY EXPERIMENTS

How to Live Freely
in a Goal-Obsessed World

ANNE-LAURE LE CUNFF

Avery
an imprint of Penguin Random House
New York

AVERY

an imprint of Penguin Random House LLC
1745 Broadway, New York, NY 10019
penguinrandomhouse.com

Book design by Angie Boutin

Library of Congress Cataloging-in-Publication Data

Names: Le Cunff, Anne-Laure, author.
Title: Tiny experiments: how to live freely in a goal-obsessed
world / Anne-Laure Le Cunff.
Description: New York: Avery, [2025] | Includes index.
Identifiers: LCCN 2024044590 (print) | LCCN 2024044591 (ebook) |
ISBN 9780593715130 (hardcover) | ISBN 9780593715147 (epub)
Subjects: LCSH: Self-actualization (Psychology)
Classification: LCC BF637.S4 L399 2025 (print) |
LCC BF637.S4 (ebook) | DDC 158.1—dc23/eng/20241025
LC record available at https://lccn.loc.gov/2024044590
LC ebook record available at https://lccn.loc.gov/2024044591

ISBN 9798217045785 (International edition)

Printed in the United States of America
1st Printing

The authorized representative in the EU for product safety and compliance is Penguin Random House Ireland, Morrison Chambers, 32 Nassau Street, Dublin D02 YH68, Ireland, https://eu-contact.penguin.ie.

To the wise teachers who always lead me back to curiosity

Contents

Don't let anyone rob you of your imagination, your creativity, or your curiosity. It's your place in the world; it's your life. Go on and do all you can with it, and make it the life you want to live.

—Mae Jemison, American engineer, physician, and former NASA astronaut

Goodbye, Linear Life

"Are you sure?" my manager asked me, with genuine concern. I was twenty-seven, living in San Francisco, and had just turned in my resignation from Google. I was voluntarily leaving what had been my dream job: amazing pay, international travel, challenging work that matched my skills, interesting colleagues, and seemingly no limit to the heights I could achieve if I continued climbing the corporate ladder. When I got this job fresh out of university, my parents were happier than I'd ever seen them. And so was I! It was a chance to be part of the heartland of the tech world.

So my manager's question made sense. No, I wasn't sure I was doing the right thing. But I didn't say that. Instead I nodded confidently, gave her a hug, and thanked her for these formative years.

The question you're probably asking is *why*.

Google's headquarters in California was an unlikely place for me to end up. I'm French Algerian and I was raised in Paris. My mother was born in Sidi Okba, Algeria, known in ancient times as "the city of magic" because of its extraordinary propensity to attract spiritual leaders. At the doors of the Sahara Desert, Sidi Okba was a gateway where Arabs and Bedouins met for the commerce of spices, camels, and fabrics. My father was born in the fortified French city of Dinan, which for many centuries was a strategic place to circulate between Normandy and Brittany. It is known for one of the largest medievalist events in Europe, where people gather to celebrate the city walls with annual themes such as "gates to the imagination" or "the times of builders."

Christmas in my family meant halal turkey and champagne. I wore miniskirts to school in France and covered my hair with a veil when visiting my family in Algeria. My father, in the French didactic tradition of mathematics, would teach me about fractals and chaos theory, while my mother would share Arabic proverbs.

Although they came from different worlds, there was one point my parents agreed on: the importance of studying hard and choosing your career wisely. I was the first woman in my family to pursue higher education, encouraged by both my father, who saw it as the path to success, and my mother, who saw it as the path to survival. My curriculum—science and business—was optimized for job prospects.

As a child of the internet, I had always been fascinated with how pixels come to life. I spent my teenage years exploring my curiosity in weird and wonderful ways: maintaining a hand-coded blog whose design changed every few weeks, translating obscure Japanese songs into French, and managing an online community for young fiction writers. Every day, millions around the world came online to learn, connect, tinker, and create. There was a sense of mystery as to how it all worked, as well as a certain reverence for the magicians at companies like Google weaving all those threads to produce the World Wide Web.

I got my Google interview in a fluke, after nerding out about the future of technology with a stranger sitting next to me on a flight to San Francisco. I went through their intense hiring process and landed the job—the perfect job. I arrived on campus feeling lucky, along with a dash of impostor syndrome.

Google is famously data-driven, so each project assigned to me had clear objectives. Career success was also codified around two tangible concepts: the ladder for your role and the level for your seniority. The promotion process was based on a rubric telling you exactly what skills you need to have demonstrated to graduate to the next level. No need to guess. No need to tinker. It was all in there, clearly mapped out.

Inspired by my peers, cheered on by my parents and my friends back in France, I set out to diligently climb the ladder. I scheduled my days in thirty-minute increments, promptly replied to all emails, volunteered for extra projects, and even found time to arrange one-to-one meetings with mentors who helped me plot the next steps in my Google career. I was flown all around the world for conferences and trade shows. I got promoted and took on a global role in the digital health team. I sometimes had to cancel social plans to work late hours on presentations, but believed it was worth the sacrifice. My journey was mapped out before me; all I had to do was keep climbing.

FROM ONE LADDER TO ANOTHER

American psychiatrist Irvin Yalom wrote about awakening experiences—events that shake us from default routines, crack our defensive barriers, and open new possibilities. Some of them can be major, such as the loss of a loved one, divorce, war, and illness. Others can be referred to as "a sort of petite existential shock therapy"—sobering thoughts that lead you to reconsider how you are really living. It took a combination of both to reawaken my consciousness.

One morning as I was getting ready for work, I noticed my arm had turned purple. I went to the Google infirmary, where I was sent to the Stanford hospital. The doctors found a blood clot that threatened to travel to my lungs. Surgery was required to remove it. I was so worried about derailing my team's ongoing projects that I asked to delay the operation so that I could time it when everyone would be off work for a company retreat. My manager would have been furious if she knew I had done this, so I didn't tell her.

When they picked me up at the hospital after the surgery, my friends snapped a group picture. I was in the middle, in a wheelchair, smiling and holding a bouquet of flowers. My face looked the same as before the surgery, but already I could feel that something had shifted in me. I recovered quickly and went back to work, kept hitting my targets and supporting my team, but my efforts felt mechanical.

Not long after, I went home to France for Christmas, my first time back in a year. I was surrounded by friends and family I hadn't seen in ages. Someone asked, "How's life?" Such a trivial question, and yet . . . When I automatically replied that work-is-great-and-San-Francisco-is-nice-thank-you, I noticed for the first time how inert my voice sounded.

How *was* life, really?

I hadn't ever asked myself this. I was too busy, always focused on finishing the next deliverable or hitting a bigger target. And I was living the dream—so of course everything must be great.

Separated from San Francisco by thousands of miles, I finally let myself honestly confront the question. Life wasn't terrible, but it wasn't great, either. I was likely burned out, but that was only a symptom of the problem. I was so consumed by the routine, the rubric, and the next rung on the ladder that I had lost the ability to notice anything else. I stopped asking what I wanted out of my day or even out of my future.

And despite this relentless grind, I was also finding myself getting bored. While I had spent my younger life guided by a genuine yearning to learn and grow, I was now following a prescribed path trodden by so many colleagues before me.

Realizing how I felt was like an electric shock. Many people are able to build a rewarding, balanced life on the foundation of a job at Google. I was not one of them. On my first day back in the office after the holiday, I quit.

In hindsight, I could have used a reflective pause after quitting, but I wasn't able to sit with the fear and anxiety of having gone from celebrated employee to unemployed nobody. My mom was already worried I was headed for the homeless shelter. So I immediately threw myself into the next socially sanctified adventure: after working at a Big Tech company to grow your professional network and save up some money, break off the golden handcuffs to build a company of your own.

I moved back to Europe and founded a tech startup.

Within a year, the young company was highlighted as one of "the healthcare startups you need to know about" in

WIRED magazine. I broke up with my first cofounder but then was accepted into a prestigious startup accelerator, where I met a new cofounder. We spent an inordinate amount of time building pitch decks and meeting with potential business partners. I was so busy, I didn't notice I had jumped from one kind of hyperfocused, outcome-driven pursuit to another.

Only when we failed to advance to the next stage of the accelerator and had to shut down the company did I allow myself to sit still for a moment. In truth, I had no choice. There was no obvious next step. After years of hustling, I finally went to a place I had never allowed my adult self to go to before: I admitted that I was lost.

And that was the most liberating thought I'd ever had.

ON THE DOORSTEP OF CHANGE

You might be familiar with the Hero's Journey, a narrative pattern first described by mythologist Joseph Campbell in his influential book *The Hero with a Thousand Faces,* one found in stories across cultures and time. We face challenges, descend into the abyss of the unknown, and must find the resources to break a path and reemerge transformed. Just like in the myths, life is made of cycles of being lost and finding ourselves again.

Feeling lost and free, I started thinking about my in-between time not as a dead end to escape, but as a space worth exploring. And with that mindset, I quickly became reacquainted with an old friend and ally: curiosity.

Not having a clear playbook to follow opened a world of possibility. I paid attention to the conversations that energized me and the topics that drew me in. I took online courses. I attended workshops. I bought books for pure pleasure. All the while, I freelanced to maintain a source of income. I felt like my old self again, and I loved her. I wasn't falling off a cliff. Rather, I was living in my own Choose Your Own Adventure novel.

My curiosity kept leading me back to the human brain. Why do we think the way we think and feel the way we feel? The more books I read, the more intrigued I became, until I eventually decided to return to school to study neuroscience. This time, I didn't have a grand plan. I just wanted to explore, learn, and grow. I was wholeheartedly stepping into the unknown.

Although I was in a formal program, I didn't want my curiosity to stop flowing. Inspired by the experimental mindset taught in scientific training, I asked myself: *What experiment could I run on my own life that would bring me an intrinsic sense of fulfillment, whatever the outcome?*

I love writing, so I made a pact with myself to write and share 100 articles in 100 workdays, drawing on my university studies and personal readings. I wrote about mental health at work, creativity, and mindful productivity.

Sharing my work daily was terrifying at first. I felt naked. I was admitting to the world that I was a work in progress, as was everything I wrote. My only anchor was the pact itself. I resisted the urge to clarify my end goal and solely focused on showing up. It wasn't always easy to do, so I leaned into self-reflection. I took notes and journaled. I watched for signs of burnout and played with various formats—such as shorter articles for when life got busy.

Slowly, a path emerged. I finished the 100 articles and decided to keep going. My newsletter grew steadily to one hundred thousand readers. I called it Ness Labs, a combination of the suffix *–ness*, which describes the quality of being (which you find in words such as *awareness, consciousness, mindfulness*), and *labs,* as I wanted it to be a laboratory for personal experimentation. People wrote emails to thank me for helping them turn chaos into creativity, for sharing tools to reduce their anxiety, and for opening doors to parts of their minds they had been afraid of exploring. Others asked if I would ever create a course or write a book.

I kept on with my studies, and today, as a neuroscientist, I investigate how different brains learn differently using technologies such as electroencephalography and eye-tracking. Ness Labs has turned into a thriving small business with an amazing team. I get to speak and write about topics I care about.

The uncertainty of my future isn't gone, and yet each day I wake up excited to discover what new crossroads life will present to me. I'm always on the lookout for new experiments. I'm not rushing to get to a specific destination. I'm playing a different game: a game of noticing, questioning, and adapting.

TOOLS FOR THE IN-BETWEENS

Uncertainty has so much to teach us. We experience it not just in big life transitions, but in lesser moments of ambiguity, such as the "messy middle" of a project, when we'd like to throw in the towel. When we find ourselves in these precarious moments, our automatic response is too often fear or anxiety. And so we rush toward a defined outcome to escape it, as I did with my startup.

But there is another way: the experimental way.

I've spent the past years at Ness Labs developing tools that help us live lives of joyful experimentation. My pact of 100 articles was the beginning of a new approach to growth—distilled in this book—based on research and what I learned teaching thousands of people how to implement its principles. Through empirical study and personal experience, I have isolated a set of practices that are an antidote to burnout and boredom alike—a counterforce to the fear, overwhelm, confusion, and loneliness many people I know are feeling as they try to apply old notions of success to the world we're living in today.

This book isn't a step-by-step recipe for accomplishing a specific goal. Rather, it offers a set of tools you can adapt to discover and achieve your own goals—especially if these goals fall outside the well-defined ambitions suggested by society.

Together, these tools will enrich your life with systematic curiosity—a conscious commitment to inhabit the space between what you know and what you don't, not with fear and anxiety but with interest and openness. Systematic curiosity provides an unshakable certitude in your ability to grow even when the exact path forward is uncertain, with the knowledge that your actions can align with your most authentic ambitions.

In the following four parts of the book, you will learn how to:

- Get started by committing to curiosity.
- Keep going by practicing mindful productivity.
- Stay flexible by collaborating with uncertainty.
- Dream bigger by growing with the world.

You are about to replace an old linear model of success with an experimental model of personal and professional growth. In this new model, your goals will be discovered, pursued, and adapted—not in a vacuum, but in conversation with the larger world. You will ask big questions and design tiny experiments to find the answers. You will become comfortable with following a nonlinear path, where each crossroads is a call for adventure.

This way of life is based on ancestral wisdom and backed by modern scientific knowledge. It shows that when you lean into your curiosity, uncertainty can be a state of expanded possibility, a space for metamorphosis. It's a way to turn challenges into triggers for self-discovery and doubt into a source of opportunity. Get ready for an exciting new era: your experimental life.

PACT

Commit to Curiosity

1

⟨?⟩ *Why Goal Setting Is Broken*

It was raining as the woman climbed out of her plane, her legs shaky from the long flight. She looked around, taking in the unfamiliar surroundings, unsure of where she was. She had landed in a big field with a beautiful view of woodland and water. This definitely didn't look like Paris, her intended destination. But she didn't have much time to enjoy the panorama; soon her plane was surrounded by hundreds of locals, curious to meet the famous Miss Amelia Earhart. When a farmer asked her, "Have you flown far?" she replied: "From America."

Yes, she had done it: though technical issues with her plane and bad weather had forced her to land in Northern Ireland, she had become the first woman to fly solo across the Atlantic.

Amelia Earhart is renowned for this incredible feat, but few people know that she had made the same trip less than five years prior, albeit in very different circumstances. Then unable to make a living as a pilot, she was working as a social worker for low-income immigrants when she received a strange phone call: She could be the first woman to fly across the Atlantic, but she would not be allowed to pilot the plane—she was to be a mere passenger. The female passenger who was initially supposed to fly with them had deemed the journey too risky.

Earhart was already an experienced aviator; she could have turned down the offer and waited for a better opportunity. But she said yes and negotiated to be in charge of the logbook so she would at least have an active role. It was this first experience that allowed her to unlock the necessary resources to try to cross the Atlantic again, this time with her own plane.

Even less known are the myriad of other experiments she performed outside of aviation. Flying was expensive, so Earhart worked as a clerk for a telephone company. She ventured into portrait photography with a friend, and when that project failed, she launched a trucking business with another friend. After she became a celebrity, she designed a functional clothing line providing comfortable yet elegant pants "for the woman who lives actively." She worked as a consultant at Purdue University to support women in pursuing traditionally male careers. She also experimented in her personal life. When she married publisher George Palmer Putnam, she told him she would not be bound by "any medieval code of faithfulness" and openly took fellow aviator Gene Vidal as a lover.

And those notes she captured during her first transatlantic flight? She published them as her first book.

We are told that success is the result of extraordinary gifts or exceptional grit. But rather than some innate quality or the single-minded pursuit of a big dream, endless curiosity is what enabled Amelia Earhart to discover her path. She saw "liking to experiment" as a common thread driving her actions in life—"the something inside me that has always liked to try new things." She was sometimes scared of failing, but she embraced her fears. She was ambitious, and yet she cared about having a positive impact. She was driven, and yet she did not focus on an end goal. She considered adventure to be worthwhile in itself. All those other facets of her life—a life of fertile uncertainty—are rarely mentioned in history books, and yet it is precisely the fact that Earhart swerved many times in the course of becoming an aviator that makes her life so extraordinary. She consistently reinvented her career, questioned the status quo, and sought to elevate others as she forged her own path.

We were all born with this sense of adventure. It's in children's nature to experiment and explore the unknown. They learn first and foremost through movement, which is considered the foundational skill for developing emotional, cognitive, and social skills. Children collect and connect information by constantly scouting their environment. They try activities beyond their capabilities, they attempt to predict the effects of their actions, and they keep asking "Why?"—in fact, children ask more than a hundred questions per hour on average. By failing fast and often, they learn from every experience to propel themselves forward. Children are insatiable adventurers.

But then something changes. We are taught to perform, in both meanings of the word: to achieve specific targets whether in school or at work, but also to present ourselves in a way that conforms with societal expectations. While some manage to preserve an attitude of childlike adventure, keeping their options open, always on the lookout for hints of what may be coming, most of us cling to what we know. When we consider our professional future, we seek a legible story, one that provides the appearance of stability, with a cohesive narrative and clear steps to success. If everything goes well, we get hired to provide answers based on our expertise—not questions based on our curiosity. We begin caring about what people think of us and we project an image of confidence, focusing on self-packaging over self-improvement. We welcome anything that provides the perception of control—whether it's a productivity tool, a time management method, or a goal-setting framework.

This common shift from boundless curiosity to narrow determination is at the heart of why the traditional approach to goals keeps on letting us down; it impedes our creativity and prevents us from seeing and seizing new opportunities.

THE TRAP OF LINEAR GOALS

Philosophers were already discussing goal setting more than two thousand years ago. "Let all your efforts be directed to something, let it keep that end in view," advised Seneca. For Epictetus, goal setting was a matter of clarity and determination: "First say to yourself what you would be, and then do what you have to do."

In the 1960s, American psychologist Edwin Locke was inspired by the work of those ancient philosophers. His goal-setting theory set off a flurry of research into the relationship between goals and performance. One of those goal-setting frameworks, devised in the early 1980s, advocated for specific, measurable, assignable, realistic, and timely goals—which you may have heard of as SMART goals.* This framework is still used to this day by thousands of companies around the world and has escaped the sphere of management to permeate the sphere of personal development.

All these approaches to goal setting are based on linear goals: they were created for controlled environments that lend to readily measurable outcomes with predictable timelines.

The linear way is wildly out of sync with the lives we live today. The challenges we're facing and the dreams we're pursuing are increasingly hard to define, measure, and pin to a set schedule. In fact, a common challenge for many people these days is feeling stuck when it comes to their next steps: instead of providing a motivating force, the idea of setting a well-defined goal is paralyzing. When the future is uncertain, the neat parameters of rigid goal-setting frameworks are of little help; it feels like throwing darts without a target to aim at.

This lack of clarity in a world that keeps on changing has led to a widespread ambivalence toward goals. As journalist Amil Niazi put it: "No goals, just vibes." Some have even proclaimed the end of ambition, a new era where the concept of job satisfaction has become a paradox.

But ambition isn't broken. It is still what it has always been: the innate human desire for growth, a desire that is both universal and highly personal. People aren't broken, either. They still crave creativity and connection. It's the way we set goals that's broken.

---

* Alternatives to these words have been proposed over time, and you might be familiar with a different version that contains, for example, *achievable* and *relevant*, or *attainable* and *resourced*.

Notice the vocabulary we use. Goals drive us *forward,* we *set out* to achieve our goals, we make progress *toward* a goal. Those are called orientational metaphors—figurative expressions that involve spatial relationships. Setting a linear goal entails defining a target state in the future and mapping out the steps to get there. Success is defined as arriving at the target.

Because they conflate ambition with the single-minded pursuit of an end destination, traditional methods of pursuing goals have an effect counter to their intent: they create a discouraging perspective where we are far from success. Our satisfaction—the best version of ourselves—lies somewhere in the future. There are (at least) three other glaring flaws of linear goals:

Linear goals stimulate fear. Starting something new is daunting, especially when it lies far outside our comfort zone. Because we lack the expertise that comes with experience, we're not sure where to begin. Sometimes the sheer number of options leads to analysis paralysis. We become so overwhelmed with choices that we are unable to take action. Other times, we feel like we're not qualified enough, and we succumb to self-doubt. We think we don't have the necessary time or financial resources. Or we may start imagining what will happen if we fail, and anxiety stops us in our tracks.

Linear goals encourage toxic productivity. Researchers who explored our relationship to idleness found that "many purported goals that people pursue may be merely justifications to keep themselves busy." Focused on relentless plotting and execution, we may develop an overly strict mentality in which we believe that if we don't complete each task, everything will fall apart. We work long hours, we feel guilty for taking breaks, we cancel on friends to do more work. We set unrealistic deadlines and blame ourselves when we miss them. We research the perfect productivity tool instead of simply asking how we feel. We work while sick. Anything to avoid slowing down on the treadmill of success. This emphasis on speed over sustainable progress leaves us mentally drained and, ironically, less productive.

Linear goals breed competition and isolation. When everyone around us is climbing the same ladder, scrambling over one another, we become competitive for all the wrong reasons. Even when we think of goals as our own individual ladder, we look at others on theirs and race toward the top. Either way, linear goals promote an individualistic mentality that can make us view potential collaborators as competitors, leading to alienation, lack of support, and fewer opportunities. The constant comparison and focus on individual achievement prevent us from pooling our resources and learning from one another, to the detriment of our careers and communities.

That is partly why *ambition* has become something of a dirty word. We assume that being ambitious means following a pre-written script and climbing a never-ending ladder, sometimes at the expense of other people. This flaw is not new, but modern life has created a giant public leaderboard that amplifies the artificial need to compete. Because of social media, we compare ourselves to our peers more than ever before. We are notified of the professional feats of not just our colleagues but all the people we studied with in school. We receive constant reminders of the supposedly perfect lives of everyone in our network. And so our definition of success keeps on ballooning as we progress.

This phenomenon is called the Red Queen effect. In *Through the Looking-Glass*, Alice says to the Queen: "In *our* country, you'd generally get to somewhere else—if you ran very fast for a long time, as we've been doing." To which the Queen replies: "A slow sort of country! Now, *here,* you see, it takes all the running *you* can do, to keep in the same place. If you want to get somewhere else, you must run at least twice as fast as that!"

Our collective focus on the ladder of success is what gave rise to the proverbial rat race of modern life: if only we can climb one more step—if only we can get that promotion, give that big presentation, grow our online audience, hire a team, buy that house—then we will finally feel at peace.

Our goals are often not even our own; we borrow them from peers, celebrities, and what we imagine society expects from us. French philosopher René Girard called this phenomenon mimetic desire: we desire something because we see others desiring it. In other words, our goals mimic the goals of others.

And of course it is impossible not to assess our game progression relative to other players—except that the leaderboard is rigged, and everyone is showing only a distorted version of their lives, snapshots of manufactured happiness where all the struggle and the doubt have been edited out.

Fear of failure causes us to endlessly stop and start, resulting in an uneven path where we keep going back to our comfort zone before trying to progress again. Toxic productivity leads to burnout, creating ups and downs. Working in isolation means we lack the support networks to help smooth the way.

Following that wild, twisted path with its intense highs and lows has repercussions. We may progress, but we feel like we're constantly failing. And so instead of inspiring audacious next steps, our goals spark anxiety (*What if I don't succeed?*), apathy (*Why care when the journey ahead is all mapped out already?*), and anger (*Why am I forced to play this game?*).

But this breakdown of old ways isn't a crisis. It's a rare chance to improve the way we explore our ambitions.

BETWEEN STIMULUS AND RESPONSE

Imagine, for a moment, that you are traveling alone on a long-leg airline flight with no onboard Wi-Fi. There you are at 30,000 feet, suspended in the sky, transitioning from one place to another, neither here nor there. The places and people who normally define and control your daily life are miles away. You don't know exactly what will happen after you land, but there's no way to rush to your destination to find out.

How do you react to this environment?

Response 1: Discomfort, fear, helplessness. The fact is, you're hurtling along at 30,000 feet in a tin can with someone else at the helm. You knock back alcohol to dull your fear or try to sleep away your anxiety. You check out to the greatest degree possible and pray to a higher power that the pilot manages to land the plane.

Or . . .

Response 2: Delight, calm, curiosity. Removed from your everyday, you find yourself relaxing—yes, even in that uncomfortable seat. In this strange space, you feel an invigorating sense of possibility. You might crack a book you've been curious about but had no time for. Watch a movie that friends would be surprised to see you enjoy. Strike up a conversation with a stranger. Maybe you write in your journal, reflecting on what's passed and mulling over what's to come. Freed from your usual duties, released from the constraints of your day-to-day identity, you find the mental space to do something a little bit different.

The flight I have just described is a liminal space—an in-between territory where the old rules governing our choices no longer apply. Life is full of these moments, and the degree to which we learn to reap their lessons is the degree to which we grow and improve our lives.

But our brain is uncomfortable in the in-betweens. We are wired to quickly label situations as good or bad, an evolutionary mechanism designed to protect us from unknown risks. Safe or not? Friend or foe? Secret passage or dead end? However, this instinct can become problematic when a clear answer isn't readily available.

Our neural activity intensifies in such situations, indicating a state of heightened arousal. Just like a sentry on high alert, the brain prepares for potential threats. Uncertainty becomes fuel for anxiety. In fact, uncertainty has been found to cause more stress than inevitable pain. When we don't know what's coming, we overthink every possibility and we conjure worst-case scenarios. Although we would like to relinquish control and soar through the skies, we often find ourselves suffering from Response 1: uneasiness, or even white-knuckled terror.

At that point, we tend to fall back on one of three defense mechanisms, where we abandon our curiosity, our ambition, or both:

- **Cynicism:** Doomscrolling, passing up opportunities, poking fun at earnest people. Like the Beast before he meets Belle, we see transformation as a source of meaningless work, and we abandon any desire to build a good life. Why suffer when we can just survive?

- **Escapism:** Retail therapy, binge watching, dream planning. Like Peter Pan, we confine ourselves to an island where we can break free from the burden of our responsibilities, an idealized place to get away from the uncertainty of our lives.

- **Perfectionism:** Self-coercion, information hoarding, toxic productivity. We treat ourselves the way the stepmother treats Cinderella—"from morning until evening, she had to perform difficult work, rising early, carrying water, making the fire, cooking and washing"—with no rest or time for ourselves.

These are not personality types. Rather, they're shields we raise in the face of uncertainty. We can shift between them depending on our circumstances.

And those defense mechanisms are perfectly normal. They're part of a cognitive process psychologists call compensatory control. When confronted with a stressful experience, our first instinct is to remove the stressor. And when we cannot eliminate the source of stress, we urgently seek activities that restore our sense of control—anything to compensate for our helplessness.

Not only are these shields we raise for protection ineffective in our modern world, but they also block our opportunities for growth, self-discovery, and what makes life exciting.

Psychologists often say that our freedom lies within the gap between stimulus and response. We can deal with the heavy load of uncertainty like the frightened flier, by closing our eyes and waiting for an unnamed pilot to land the plane— or we could make a brave go at exploring the possibilities of this in-between space.

As Amelia Earhart once said: "The most difficult thing is the decision to act." Though we may not have all the information at hand, we can choose movement instead of stagnation, exploration instead of paralysis. And when we do, the sky is just the beginning. This is the promise of an experimental mindset.

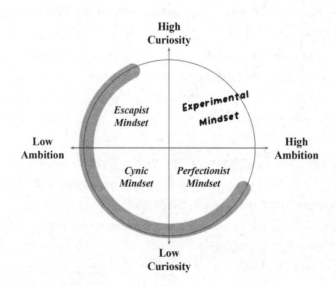

THREE MENTAL SHIFTS

How can you go from rigid linearity to fluid experimentation? Throughout this book, you will build a toolkit to support three profound shifts in how you navigate the world:

From Response 1 to Response 2. Response 1 is automatic and rooted in the anxiety of uncertainty. Response 2 is autonomous and based on a strong sense of agency. We all oscillate between the two responses, but the more we flex our curiosity muscles, the more uncertainty transforms from something to escape to somewhere to explore. Switching from Response 1 to Response 2 is switching from defensive to proactive. Instead of being passive passengers along for the ride, we can explore possibilities within the uncertainty. Not knowing the destination sparks our imagination. Freed from the need to control the outcome, we can experiment and play.

From fixed ladders to growth loops. Relying on a mental model of traditional goal setting means the focus is on linear progression toward a predefined outcome. Each rung represents a measurable achievement, a predictable step along a planned trajectory, which leaves little room for surprise or serendipity. When we shift to a "loop" mental model, the journey follows iterative cycles of experimentation, with each loop building on the last. Our task becomes to widen each loop by nurturing our creativity and leaning into promising tangents instead of dismissing them as distractions.

From outcome to process. When we are operating with an outcome-based definition of success, progress means ticking off big, hairy, audacious goals. When we shift to a process-based definition, progress is driven by incremental experimentation. Success transforms from a fixed target to an unfolding path. Without a fixed definition of success, we welcome change as a source of reinvention. Our direction emerges organically as we systematically examine what captures our attention instead of fixating on an artificial scorecard.

Linear goals promise certainty—if we just stick to the plan and climb, we will arrive safely at the expected destination. But life rarely follows such rigid and predictable patterns. Experiments are built for the in-betweens; they propel you forward even without a fixed destination, in constant conversation with your inner self and the outer world. By having the courage to leave the shore, we trade the illusion of control for the possibility of discovery. Rather than resisting uncertainty, we befriend it. The first step is to rekindle your curiosity to imagine new possibilities.

2

≣ *Escaping the Tyranny of Purpose*

Many of us believe that everything we do in life must follow a coherent story toward some ultimate purpose. In recent years, society has become obsessed with purpose-driven careers, grounded on the idea that we're each put here to serve some unique calling. In books, the popularity of the phrase *find your purpose* has surged by more than 700 percent over the past two decades.

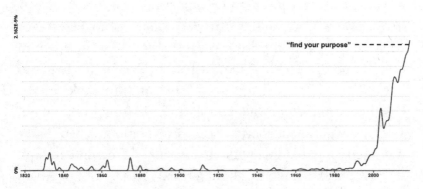

Book mentions of "find your purpose" between 1819 and 2019.

The search for purpose is often positioned as an alternative to following a conventional, conformist, or self-serving career path. I would argue that it merely replaces one kind of conformity with another. In focusing on purpose, we think we are carving a unique path, when in reality—as you will learn in this chapter—we only limit our potential for growth and learning.

Ron Finley is one person whose life would have been greatly diminished if he had held tightly to the idea that his professional life had a singular purpose that he needed to doggedly pursue. Finley first made a name for himself as a Los Angeles–based clothing designer with a collection that was sold in some of the largest retail stores across the country. He had entered fashion because he felt there weren't enough designers designing clothes specifically tailored for people of color. You could call it a passion project, with impressive commercial success. Then a recession hit. Stores stopped calling and the path to becoming a master tailor—his dream at the time—was not a viable option anymore.

Around that time, Finley started getting really annoyed at having to travel for miles to find healthy produce. It was easier to buy street drugs than organic tomatoes. His neighborhood, South Central Los Angeles, was a food desert—or what he calls a food prison, because one had to escape it in order to access healthy food. Instead of driving for hours to buy a tomato, he decided to grow fruits and vegetables on the land between the sidewalk and the curb in front of his house.

This experiment soon became a revolution. When Finley was cited for gardening without a permit, he fought back and started a petition, which ultimately led the City of Los Angeles to change the law. He was invited to give a TED talk, which gave rise to the guerrilla gardening movement—positioning urban gardening as a revolutionary act, a liberation from a broken food system.

When Finley and I connected on a video call—him in Los Angeles, me in London—he walked me through the garden. What had started as an intention to grow some tomatoes had flourished into a communal Eden: "That's a pear tree. That's an orange tree. That's compost here. We got figs, pomegranates, tangerines, apricots, and apples. We put banana trees there a year ago and they're starting to fruit," he told me as he strolled along on the sidewalk in front of his house.

As is often the case, success begets success: Finley's unplanned renown as a green leader has opened new doors for the fashion career that once seemed dormant. So now he's both a designer and an educator—and a father, an activist, an artist, and who knows what else. Being part of several tribes, each reflecting a facet of his complex identity (which psychologists call self-complexity), has made him infinitely more secure. Unlike a large but diffuse network, these tight-knit communities provide a stable support system, anchoring him in times of uncertainty in any one sphere.

Finley's story exemplifies a beautiful truth: We each have within us unlimited possibilities; purpose is therefore never a singular discovery. Life is a continuous opportunity. As Finley puts it:

> *When people ask me what I do for a living, I tell them I breathe—I'm a professional breather. We create those false transitions, we make it all look like it's separate, just like we separate a garden, from a state, from a country, and ourselves from nature. I didn't go from fashion to gardening to being a humanitarian. As a gardener, I was already a humanitarian. When I'm designing, I'm*

still a gardener. I'm still creative. And I'm still a father.
Even if you go from being a doctor to being an author.
For me, this is about freedom. It's all already within us.

In his MasterClass, he encourages students to design the life they want to lead, a life made of twists and turns that make it their life, not the linear life that's predesigned for them—a life that makes for a good story.

When thinking about your life, pretend you want to craft a captivating story. Instead of a Greek tragedy with strict creative conventions, imagine that you want to write the beginning of an unputdownable tale, the kind that breaks free from well-trodden narratives. Screenwriter Leslie Dixon, who wrote *Mrs. Doubtfire,* says there is only one rule of screenwriting: "Does the reader want to turn the page?"

When we fixate on finding one singular purpose, we rule out the side quests that help us grow the most. Your life doesn't need to follow predictable acts and arcs. The best stories are full of surprises, with colorful characters and unexpected plot twists. To avoid recycling old stories, we need to break free from the scripts we write for ourselves.

THE SHACKLES OF COGNITIVE SCRIPTS

The educator and political leader John W. Gardner wrote, "As we mature we progressively narrow the scope and variety of our lives. Of all the interests we might pursue, we settle on a few. Of all the people with whom we might associate, we select a small number. We become caught in a web of fixed relationships. We develop set ways of doing things."

In a seminal 1979 study, cognitive scientists asked participants to describe the components of a particular "scene," such as going to the doctor. Participants largely produced the same responses, mentioning similar characters, props, and actions, as well as the order in which these actions should occur: checking in with the receptionist, reading magazines in the waiting room, getting their name called . . .

Since then, researchers have expanded on this idea, discovering a virtually infinite number of internalized patterns that govern our thoughts, actions, and decision-making—from work to relationships and education—giving rise to a branch of cognitive science known as Cognitive Script Theory.

Just as we have a sense of how we should behave when visiting a doctor and how the events there should unfold (we'd be alarmed if we were asked to undress in the waiting room), we also have a sense of how things "should" play out in other areas of our lives. When we navigate the world, the brain attempts to match the information it receives with a similar representation it already has in memory: a cognitive script.

Cognitive scripts offer a predictable mold where the outcomes are clearly defined and the benefits pre-agreed. They act like programmed instructions that we follow in certain situations based on our past experiences. We follow these scripts because they provide us with a sense of confidence: established norms and predictable patterns reduce the fear of the unknown. We also tend to feel more confident when we act in ways that align with societal expectations, since it increases the chance that our choices and actions will be validated and reinforced by others around us.

It is reassuring to think that we have a good sense of how things "should" turn out, and it is useful not to be overwhelmed by every new situation so that we can make daily decisions. But these cognitive scripts can also become shackles confining us within artificial boundaries, limiting our perception of what is possible. Their insidious influence can lead us to ambitions that are really just adjuncts to the old linear goals we've clung to. There are myriads of cognitive scripts, but I see three broad categories surfacing as people consider their next steps: the Sequel, the Crowdpleaser, and the Epic.

THE SEQUEL SCRIPT: WHEN WE FOLLOW OUR PAST

We think that our life should be a continuous journey toward a single purpose. These established paths are like ruts—rails excavated over time that guide vehicles along an already-marked course. Imagine a horse-drawn cart arriving at a crossroads with deep ruts. If the ruts go right, the driver will have a very difficult time turning left.

While it's undeniable that our past influences our future, we can create an artificial sense of purpose by placing more rigid limits on ourselves than actually exist, trying our best to make our decisions conform with our past behaviors. We effectively keep on writing sequels based on previous experiences.

The Sequel script is based on a phenomenon that is so widespread it has many names. Psychologists refer to it as the continuation bias, economists talk of path dependence, and philosophers might frame it as a form of fatalism. I call this phenomenon the self-consistency fallacy: the assumption that "I have always acted in a certain way; therefore, I must continue to act in this way."

If the next logical step after business school is to join a consultancy company, it might feel like too much of a departure to start your own small consulting business when you graduate. If the conventional path is to finish high school and immediately enroll in college, it won't be an obvious next step to take a gap year to travel or volunteer. If Ron Finley had followed the Sequel script, he might have walked away from the gardening fight, feeling like it diverged too far from the career he had spent years building.

The Sequel script is why we maintain the same roles and behaviors in our relationships, such as always being the "quiet one" in our circle of friends even when we feel a desire to express ourselves more openly. It makes us cling to our past successes, trying to repeat them. It limits our imagination by making us rehash old tales instead of facing the discomfort of a blank page.

THE CROWDPLEASER SCRIPT: WHEN WE FOLLOW THE CROWD

For Ron Finley, being a famous fashion designer was a socially sanctioned form of success. On the other hand, as you can imagine, the role of "guerrilla gardener" did not automatically confer the same level of status.

Unless you live in complete isolation, you will inevitably experience pressure from those around you to conform to established definitions of success, or merely to their own personal definition. Adjusting your decisions to meet the expectations of a group is a deeply ingrained behavior, which can be driven by the fear of social exclusion or a sense of guilt about following a different path. Neuroimaging studies have shown that the same part of the brain that deals with conflict is active when our choices differ from those of the group.

Some paths come with more prestige embedded in them than others. Doctor, lawyer, and professor are some of the obvious ones, but a greater status can also be attached to the name of a company, a higher salary, or even a location, such as getting a job in the city when you've grown up in a small town.

Although your friends, family, and colleagues may not explicitly push you toward a specific career, society at large has ingrained in us certain standards we can't help but measure ourselves against. These standards take the form of milestones you feel are crucial to your story: finishing school, getting a job, meeting a partner, starting a family.

When you deviate from what is commonly perceived as the most sensible path, anxious questions often follow, both from within yourself and from others: Shouldn't you focus on your studies instead of working on a side project? Are you sure you want to switch careers when you have a mortgage? Is it reasonable to start over in a new city at your age?

My mother was terrified when I told her I was going to leave my job at Google. I was jumping into the unknown while renouncing a prestigious and, most importantly, secure job many people aspired to. It took years for her anxiety to subside—and only after I had proven I could keep a roof over my head and food on the table.

Nobody likes to worry their loved ones, and social conformity may seem to offer the path of least resistance. But it isn't without costs. For the sake of external validation or simply to appease other people, you may find yourself following the Crowdpleaser script and pursuing a conformist path instead of following your curiosity. You might live a dream life, but whose dream is it?

THE EPIC SCRIPT: WHEN WE FOLLOW OUR PASSION

Even if we perform the miraculous feat of freeing ourselves from the past and from the crowd, we face the risk of falling prey to another type of script, which is omnipresent on our bookshelves: "Do what you love!" "Chase your dreams!" "Follow your passion!"

This is the most acute manifestation of our obsession with purpose: a deceptive "ideal" path that is contrived around some imagined destination that is far from where we currently stand. This is yet another linear goal, focused more on the target than on the journey. Ron Finley managed to be successful, for a while, turning his childhood passion into a career as a designer. But far more often, Epic scripts end the way mine did when I quit my job to build a purpose-driven startup: in failure.

The popularity of the Epic script is largely due to survivorship bias, when we mistake a successful subgroup as the entire group, overlooking those who failed. This phenomenon is particularly common in entrepreneurship, where we try to emulate the success of a few successful founders without realizing that the purpose-driven narrative they promote doesn't take all the other factors involved—luck, money, support network—into account.

Of course, the Epic script is painfully pointless if, like many people, you don't have a clear existing passion to follow. And for those who do have a passion, the Epic script narrows the options they may explore. The idea that people find their purpose fully developed implies that we have only a limited number of potential callings, which can cause people to neglect other interesting paths.

The Epic script also implies that following your passion will automatically lead to success, which makes any difficulty much harder to manage. Stanford psychologist Carol Dweck and colleagues found that mantras like "find your passion" increase the likelihood that people will give up on their newfound interest when they run into inevitable hurdles. As they write in the paper: "Urging people to find their passion may lead them to put all their eggs in one basket but then to drop that basket when it becomes difficult to carry."

By making you dream too big, the Epic script can keep you from performing small but meaningful experiments that could open unexpected doors. It may also lead you to opt for needlessly risky experiments when a smaller, safer version of the same experiment would have yielded sufficient data.

CAN YOU EVEN hear yourself when so many voices tell you what to do next? In the thicket of all those exhortations to write your story within the well-defined conventions of cognitive scripts, it's easy to become disconnected from yourself and your curiosity. Fortunately, just like you have learned these scripts, you can unlearn them.

UNLEARNING YOUR SCRIPTS

Alvin Toffler, the futurist who coined the term *information overload* in the 1970s, wrote that the illiterate of our times will not be those who cannot read and write, but those who cannot learn, unlearn, and relearn. In Japanese Noh theater, performers are told to transcend mere imitation of the techniques they learned in order to attain a deeper, more spontaneous expression of their art. Similarly, before you can relearn to experiment and turn life into the giant playground it ought to be, you need first to unlearn your cognitive scripts.

The beauty of shifting from linear goals to experiments is that you don't have to force your decisions to fit into any notion of who you thought you were or wanted to be. You are allowed to go off script. You can have multiple passions. You can make progress without a fixed purpose.

As you consider your next experiment, three questions can help you avoid the trap of the Sequel, the Crowdpleaser, and the Epic and reclaim your cognitive freedom:

- Are you following your *past* or discovering your *path*?

- Are you following the *crowd* or discovering your *tribe?*

- Are you following your *passion* or discovering your *curiosity?*

A little unlearning is a dangerous thing. Equipped with these principles, you can actively challenge your cognitive scripts and rewrite your own narrative to design a life that's truly experimental. Because the world is changing and so are you, you can play with the rules and decide which question genuinely piques your curiosity.

AN ANTHROPOLOGY OF YOUR LIFE

The number one barrier to self-renewal is not lack of time or lack of money; it's not knowing how to begin. Should I keep my current job or take a risk and start my own business? Should I stay in my hometown or move to a new city? Should I pursue further education or focus on gaining more work experience? These questions can be paralyzing, but they can also be the seed of discovery. All it takes is the courage to be curious.

As you've seen, it is possible to break free from cognitive scripts and carve your own path—but it requires a hard reset. In the words of the twentieth-century economist and philosopher John Maynard Keynes: "The difficulty lies, not in the new ideas, but in escaping the old ones, which ramify, for those brought up as most of us have been, into every corner of our minds."

To escape those old ideas, think of yourself as an anthropologist with your own life as your topic of study. Anthropology requires "the open-mindedness with which one must look and listen, record in astonishment and wonder that which one would not have been able to guess."

Anthropologists ask fundamental questions such as: What does it mean to live in our world as a human being? How can the study of humanity reveal new ways of being human and help us imagine our collective future? In search of answers, they conduct *fieldwork*: They go into the field and write field notes. These notes could be written observations, or they may take the form of visual maps to chart relationships and uncover intriguing connections.

For just one day, I invite you to play a game of self-anthropology. It's a game of curiosity, an exercise in receptiveness, a way to deactivate your cognitive scripts. It's a fun opportunity to conduct an audit of your life and reevaluate your goals.

There is no need for fancy tools or scientific equipment. Simply create a new note on your phone so you can jot down thoughts as you go about your day. Call it "Field Notes" or another title that feels playful or meaningful. Then, whenever something crosses your mind, write a time stamp and a few words.

To capture representative data, you should ideally do this exercise on a typical workday. You might write something down after you read an inspiring article or listen to an infuriating podcast, record a thought-provoking phrase from a conversation with a friend or capture your feeling after they have left. Maybe you put down an idea that comes to you on the train or the feelings you had minutes before giving an important presentation.

The aim is not to create a lengthy narrativized record of your day or to keep a meticulous log akin to calorie counting. Don't try to capture everything. Use your curiosity as a compass.

Field notes offer a way to become an active observer and to discover interesting patterns in your life. Because you take notes in the present moment, rather than waiting until the end of the day to reflect, you're less likely to forget bursts of inspiration and fleeting ideas that might otherwise get lost in the bustle of the day.

When you collect lots of small data points, you create a "breadcrumb trail" and are more likely to notice overarching trends than if you were to focus only on the most salient experiences. Because of the time stamps, you'll easily be able to remember where you were.

There are no limitations as to what you can include in your field notes. Here are some ideas to inspire you:

- **Insights:** Your moments of curiosity, random thoughts, new ideas, and questions that spark your interest.

- **Energy:** Your shifts in energy levels throughout the day, as well as what gives you energy or drains your energy.

- **Mood:** Your emotions during or after an experience, whether it's a meeting, a workout, a podcast, etc.

- **Encounters:** Your social interactions or new connections and any insights or feelings that arose from them.

To augment those written notes, you might additionally create a photo album where you store images of things, places, or people that jumped out at you, or a sketchbook for drawing and doodling. Just as anthropologists have many ways of capturing their observations, be creative and let your preferred modes of expression determine the scope and shape of your field notes.

As a record of your activities, thoughts, and emotions, your field notes will serve as a rich source of observations that you can then turn into insights to guide the selection of your next experiment. After just twenty-four hours, you will have a treasure trove of data about a typical day in your life. Spend time reading your notes and reflecting. Look for recurring themes, interesting details, and general feelings that come up again and again.

This is a fluid process. You may notice categories for "things that give me joy" and "things that drain me," or for "what I want more of" and "what I want less of," or big categories for important aspects of your life such as learning, relationships, and health.

Simply by grouping your breadcrumbs into larger piles, you will see patterns emerge. This could be a persistent challenge or a point of curiosity. For instance, you could notice that you have the morning blues every day when it's time to go to work or that your moods tend to be higher when you participate in group projects. It could be that a specific type of task always makes you feel creative or that conversations with certain people tend to yield more insights. Maybe every time you read about a specific topic, you wish you knew more about it.

Data can also tell you a lot through what is *not* there. Pay attention to invisible gaps and curiosity attractors: When you take a step back to consider a typical day of your life, do you feel like anything is missing? Do you feel a yearning toward something different?

Like a scientist, you can now use your observations to formulate a hypothesis. It all starts with a research question. For example, if you observe that you're feeling energized when discussing certain topics, you might ask yourself: *How can I incorporate more of this into my daily life?*

Then turn this question into a hypothesis. Don't overthink it. Formulating a hypothesis is an intuitive process based on your past experiences and present inclinations. It should simply be an idea you want to put to the test—an inkling of an answer to your research question.

If you observed that you dread giving presentations, maybe improv classes could help build your confidence. If you feel anxious in the morning, maybe meditation could help regulate your emotions. If you enjoy graphic design, maybe freelancing could help you strengthen your portfolio.

OBSERVATION	QUESTION	HYPOTHESIS
I'm dreading giving presentations.	How can I become more confident?	Improv classes might build my confidence.
I feel anxious in the morning.	How can I feel more grounded before going to work?	Meditation might help regulate my emotions.
I get excited when talking about renewable energy.	How can I learn more about the renewable energy sector?	Networking with professionals might open new doors.
I rarely have time to read.	How can I make reading a part of my daily life?	Setting aside specific times might help me build a reading habit.
I enjoy graphic design and receive positive feedback on my work.	How can I do more graphic design work?	Freelancing might be a fun way to strengthen my portfolio.

Notice how different each question and its corresponding hypothesis are from linear goals. In the work-related examples above, the ultimate aim is not to become a successful public speaker or graphic designer. Rather than an attempt to reach a fixed destination, testing a hypothesis is an opportunity for growth. You are simply exploring your potential, driven by genuine curiosity, asking yourself: *What might I find on that path?* Once you have a hypothesis, you can design an experiment and turn your life into a giant laboratory for self-discovery.

3

❦ *A Pact to Turn Doubts*
into Experiments

Alexander Kallaway was once a typical high school student in Russia. He had a quiet life, but the world called to him: What new cultures and customs might he discover if he left this familiar environment? What skills could he gain by learning from different perspectives?

So he found a way to study at a Japanese university and, once he had his degree, attended business school in Canada. After graduation, he started a career in digital marketing in his newly adopted home country. Work was going great, but he soon noticed he was missing a core entrepreneurial skill: if he wanted to collaborate with developers, he needed to learn how to code. Kallaway had already accumulated several loans to study abroad, so he could not afford to go back to school for a computer science degree. Instead, he decided to teach himself after work using free online resources.

Staying committed was hard. When it wasn't the lure of Toronto, a fun, vibrant city with many opportunities to explore, it was the temptation to stay home and watch TV. So he created an accountability group. Kallaway simply committed to showing up and hosting study sessions at local coffee shops, but the group quickly outgrew those facilities and moved to a coworking space. What started as a small study group became one of the largest communities of developers in Canada. This was already an amazing accomplishment, but Kallaway's hard work paid off even more when he was offered his first developer position.

At that point, it would have been easy for him to take things for granted. He had an enjoyable job, made good money, and knew a lot of interesting people. But Kallaway noticed that his progress was stalling. Until he had an idea: What if he made a public oath to devote at least an hour to coding every day for the next three months—and why not round it up to a hundred days?

This public oath was a pact: a pledge to engage in a particular activity for a predetermined period of time. The #100DaysOfCode challenge, as he came to name it, would serve as a commitment device, encouraging Kallaway to code each day after work, even when he'd rather watch TV. Not only would it keep him excited, but he would also, hopefully, learn more about himself and connect with other people in the process.

By the time the 100 days were over, Kallaway had not only become a better coder but had inspired many others to commit to their own challenge. He is now at the center of a global community of thousands of developers, all learning and growing together.

How can you, just like Kallaway, transform your life into a giant laboratory—a playground where doubt is a source of inspiration and experimentation?

DESIGNING A TINY EXPERIMENT

By unlearning your cognitive scripts, collecting data on your life, and brainstorming potential hypotheses to test, you have already reawakened your perception of what is possible. Thanks to your field notes, you are now ready to design an experiment that doesn't fall into the trap of linear thinking. The final step is to turn your hypothesis into a pact—an actionable commitment you will fulfill for a set period of time.

A pact is a simple and repeatable activity that will inevitably bring you closer to achieving your authentic ambitions, regardless of the actual result of each trial. It follows a simple format:

I will [action] for [duration].

The pact is the fundamental building block of personal experimentation, a self-invitation to try something new and learn from the experience. It's a call to escape inertia and live in forward motion. What makes a pact so effective is that it focuses on your outputs (e.g., "publish 25 newsletters over the next 25 weeks") rather than your outcomes (e.g., "get 5,000 newsletter subscribers in 25 weeks"). It gives you the confidence to get started because there is no bad result or wrong choice. You just need to show up. A pact is:

- **Purposeful.** Although it frees you from fixating on the outcome, a pact should still feel exciting and provide meaning through the learning journey itself. When each experiment is purposeful, there is no need for a grand life purpose.

- **Actionable.** A good experiment is based on actions you can reliably perform. Your pact should be doable with your current resources, so you can take action today rather than overplan for tomorrow.

- **Continuous.** For the collection of consistent data, it's important that the action that constitutes your pact is simple and repeatable. For instance, your pact could be something you do every day, every weekend, or every week.

- **Trackable.** Notice I don't say *measurable* here. Performance metrics can make you focus on the outcome. Instead, you should be able to track your pact with a binary question: Have you done it or not? Yes or no? This makes your progress easy to monitor.

Compared to linear goals, a pact fosters an experimental mindset—an attitude of openness and curiosity, a willingness to learn with a sense of receptiveness, and a lack of preconceived notions. When we play with problems, they become a sandbox where we can experiment and relinquish control over the outcome, just like a scientist who keeps a neutral stance when observing the results and taking notes to tweak future iterations.

Any uncertainty or curiosity can be turned into a pact, from exploring a new hobby to learning a new skill, gauging a potential career path, or trying out a new routine. A pact can be easy, such as two weeks of daily stretching, or it can be more ambitious, such as creating a digital illustration every week for the next three months. It can help you test your assumptions when it comes to your work (e.g., blocking two hours for reading and creative thinking on Mondays for a month), your health (e.g., going to bed at the same time every day for a week), or your relationships (e.g., date night with your spouse every other Saturday for six months).

We have very little control over how we feel, which is why it's hard to force ourselves to feel motivated. A pact solves this challenge by emphasizing *doing* over *planning*. As psychologist and philosopher William James explained: "Action seems to follow feeling, but really action and feeling go together; and by regulating the action, which is under the more direct control of the will, we can indirectly regulate the feeling, which is not."

Just like the protocol of a scientific experiment, a pact is based on instructions that are clear and contained. That's why "I will learn how to code" is a flawed pact, but "I will code every day for a hundred days" is a great one. Instead of "I will write a book," try "I will write every weekday for the next six months." Replace "I will run a marathon" with "I will run every Sunday for six weeks." The format of the pact provides a simple mechanism to commit to action, a way to rely on momentum instead of motivation. You just need to get started and trust that you will naturally build confidence through repetition.

THE POWER OF REPEATED TRIALS

Khe Hy worked on Wall Street for fifteen years and thought he had fulfilled dreams he had held since childhood: income, status, a nice apartment. But deep inside, he felt numb and was afraid he'd spend the rest of his life going through the motions. So he left and created a blog. "As I started to write and to become an internet creator," he told me, "I committed to trying things out for one-month experiments. I'm going to try Snapchat for a month and see what happens, or I'm going to try a podcast for fifty-two weeks."

Notice the specific number of repetitions. Committing in advance to a specific duration for your experiment has an obvious advantage: it forces you to wait until after a pre-agreed number of iterations before making a decision. This will make you less likely to abandon your pact because of one particularly challenging week. You can remain confident even when facing unexpected hurdles along the way.

Confidence isn't a quality we are born with or something that magically happens; it's built through action. To create confidence, you need to get started. Every time you act, you bet on yourself and gather evidence that you can do what you set out to do.

Repeated trials are an essential feature of experiments. You need enough trials to obtain results you can trust. Imagine you and your friend are playing darts and want to know who aims better. You can't claim to be the best dart player based on a single throw. You need to throw the dart multiple times to see if you consistently hit the bull's-eye or if it was just a lucky shot. Similarly, you cannot decide if you would like to live in a city by spending one afternoon there, and you cannot know whether people enjoy your writing by publishing just one essay. A good experiment requires multiple trials to confirm that the results are not just due to chance.

The repeated trials of your pact provide you with more reliable information to make decisions. Furthermore, each iteration is likely to be more successful, fueling growth in its own right regardless of whether you opt to extend your pact beyond its initial period.

This tendency for later responses to a creative problem to be better than earlier ones is called the serial-order effect, which is considered "one of the oldest and most robust findings in modern creativity work." Put simply, it pays off to iterate.

Although the serial-order effect is most evident in short-term tasks, creativity can be nurtured over the course of a lifetime. The myth of startup success often emphasizes youth. But the odds of a founder in their fifties reaching a successful exit are almost double those of a founder in their thirties. Similar patterns apply to creative breakthroughs in science. The peak productivity of a scientist occurs around the age of forty.

Of course, early success is fascinating because it's unusual, but the most reliable way to be successful is to try, fail, learn, and try again. That's why so many successful startups and scientific inventions are created by people in their forties and older: they've put in more reps—they went through more trials to learn from their mistakes.

How many repetitions do you need to benefit from the serial-order effect? Expertise can take decades of steady practice. And the longer the pact, the more likely you are to quit before completing it. Fortunately, you are not aiming for long-term competency, just immediate confidence in your next steps.

In general, more repetitions will give you more data. You are unlikely to gain life-changing insights in a couple of days. In the words of John Maxwell: "The more you do, the more you fail. The more you fail, the more you learn. The more you learn, the better you get." But this works only if you actually complete each loop, so keep your commitment realistic. There's no point in making a three-month commitment if you give up after a few days.

Shorter time frames are often more effective. For something completely new that you have never tried before, a ten-day pact is a good starting point. This provides enough time to start noticing patterns while not being overly intimidating. If it is something you have experimented with previously, then a one-month pact allows you to build on that familiarity. Finally, for activities that are already part of your life but which you wish to engage in more regularly, a three-month pact helps reinforce and amplify patterns so you can collect better quality data to guide your journey. Incidentally, three months is roughly the length of the #100DaysofCode challenge and my own challenge of writing 100 articles in 100 workdays at Ness Labs.

Please don't let these suggestions deter you from a longer pact. Sarah Tate, a former Google colleague of mine, gave herself twelve months to explore whether coaching could be a fulfilling career path. "I had a hypothesis that as a coach, I could do what I love in my way, and make enough money for our needs," she explained. "So I gave myself a year to experiment with my hypothesis." After ten months, she knew this was the right path for her at that moment.

Your time frame can even be a preliminary indicator of your interest in an experiment. Are you willing to commit for this duration to explore this path? If you're exhausted just thinking about it, then you will be better off crafting a more achievable pact. Remember: The value of a pact lies not in its length but in the insights and growth it brings.

WHAT A PACT IS NOT

Because of the emphasis on repeated action, a pact could be confused with other tools for goal setting and behavior change. So let me clarify those differences:

A pact is not a habit. A habit has an unbounded time commitment (e.g., exercise every day) driven by the desire to achieve a specific result (e.g., a positive health outcome). Failure is not the end of the world, but it's a holdback and we try to get back on track. On the other hand, a pact has a specific number of trials (e.g., write 100 articles) and is driven by curiosity (e.g., trial a writing career). Failure is a valuable source of data to help us adjust our path or even altogether abandon the pact if it's not a good fit for our ambitions. In fact, a pact can be useful *before* you decide on a new habit. We are more likely to stick to a habit if it's rewarding. But how do you know what feels right if you haven't experimented with different ways to implement the habit? Through cycles of experimentation, a pact can turn into a habit when you find it has become ingrained in your daily life in a way that goes beyond the initial commitment. For example, I started journaling as part of a two-week pact to explore mindfulness practices. Experimenting helped me find the perfect method and time of the day, and I have now been journaling every day for over three years.

A pact is not a New Year's resolution. If you've been struggling to maintain your New Year's resolutions, it's not just you. There is overwhelming evidence that New Year's resolutions don't work. A survey of over 31 million activities by the team at Strava found that most New Year's resolutions are abandoned by January 12, which they called Quitter's Day. New Year's resolutions fail because people overcommit to a bunch of lofty aspirations. The human mind has a love/hate relationship with effort. We are drawn to the idea of it, yet we would rather not have to put in actual effort. This phenomenon is known as the effort paradox. Because we mistakenly believe that we would be happier after overcoming a greater challenge, we tend to select difficult paths precisely because they require more effort—even if it means we are more likely to fail! In contrast, a pact consists of one simple action repeated over a predetermined amount of time. Many internet challenges, such as #The100DayProject or #100DaysOfCode, for instance, last less than a third of a year—a more reasonable commitment than most New Year's resolutions.

A pact is not a performance metric. When I worked at Google, we had OKRs, which stands for Objectives and Key Results. Other companies use KPIs, or Key Performance Indicators. These are all designed to achieve specific targets. Instead of the outcome, a pact focuses on the output. Success is showing up, regardless of the end result. As Ali Abdaal, who studied medicine for six years at Cambridge University before becoming a full-time online entrepreneur, told me: "I try my very best not to think about the numbers. Any time I do think about the numbers, I become burnt out. I feel like this is not fun anymore. But whenever I reaffirm that my only job is to show up, then that's what keeps me going." Instead of worrying about how he was going to survive outside the clear and defined path of a medical career, he trusted that he would find a way. Today, his YouTube channel has millions of subscribers. Changing his relationship to performance was crucial in achieving sustainable success: "People say you need to set SMART goals," he told me. "But I never set goals that are outside of my control. I just need to publish one or two videos every week."

A pact is not a resource-intensive project. As we will see in chapter 5, there are indeed resources you need to manage to complete your experiments, but these are not time and money. Experiments can be quick—for instance, just ten minutes a day for ten days. And although certain experiments may require a certain level of financial freedom, many can be conducted for free. You could experiment with meditating, running, writing, taking photos, giving presentations at work, learning how to code, playing games with your kids. You could even experiment with doing nothing for a few minutes a day.

In essence, a pact is a mini protocol for a personal experiment. It tells you what to do and how many times you will conduct the test. Not only does it provide a way to rekindle your curiosity, but it's a guarantee of growth and discovery.

HOW TO CHOOSE YOUR PACT

With your curiosity running high, beware of the maximalist brain when choosing your pact. Beyond the effort paradox, two well-established cognitive biases cause us to gravitate toward the most ambitious version of a project. The overconfidence effect, in tandem with the planning fallacy—in which we consistently underestimate the time, resources, and effort needed to finish a project—can trick us into thinking we are more capable of completing a task than we actually are. This can lead us to bite off more than we can chew.

If you are hesitating between two versions of a pact, think *tiny*: What's the smallest version of this experiment that you can run? It's easy to maintain your pact on your best days, but think instead of your worst days. For instance, actor and writer Henri Brugère first committed to publishing 250 words of scriptwriting a day. Only once he'd gained confidence in the process did he expand his pact to include videos of himself reading the scripts.

It may also be tempting to pursue several pacts at the same time, especially if you have never run such personal experiments before. As you will learn in this book, once you approach life with a spirit of playful experimentation, there will be infinite opportunities to explore interesting paths—and so there's no rush to get started with all your ideas at once.

When Corin Delgay's scented candles business failed, he learned the hard way that he didn't enjoy running numbers and balance sheets. Throughout this venture, however, multiple people had praised his ability to think creatively. So Delgay decided to explore his artistic side through a tiny experiment: "I said, let me paint twenty paintings without trying to create a masterpiece." The first paintings were far from perfect, but he remained committed to his daily practice, using online tutorials to refine each version. "I was just looking for mistakes to learn from," he told me. "It came from a place of no ego and the confidence that I would get better over time."

After only three weeks, he put together an event where he sold five paintings. Today his little gallery in Barcelona is a thriving business, with art aficionados visiting from all around the world. And Delgay still paints every day, often in public from the gallery or at live events around the city. "Once you have this positive momentum, it doesn't feel like work."

You also don't need to quit your job to conduct your experiment full time. Albert Einstein conducted most of his research while being employed as a patent examiner. Haruki Murakami wrote his first two books while running a jazz club.

Creative producer Valentin Loredo also kept his job while exploring other interests. Growing up in a family where food was a big part of life, he'd always enjoyed cooking to relax after long days at work. He felt keen to invest in his cooking skills but didn't want to sacrifice other aspects of his personal and professional life. "I have a job that takes up a lot of time, I like to travel, I like to go out," he told me. "But I liked the idea of getting back to learning and indulging in the joy of personal growth." He signed up for an online course and committed to spending three to five hours every weekend cooking in his small kitchen in Paris. "I tried new ways of doing things, I searched online when I was stuck, I'd take photos and write down notes. I focused on improving and tweaking a little bit every time. And in the evening, I'd invite my friends for a full-course dinner so that they could taste the result."

After a year and a half, he successfully passed the exam for one of the most rigorous culinary training courses in France. He has no specific plans for what he will do with the certificate. "It opened a world of possibilities. Maybe in ten years I will open a restaurant, maybe not, but these skills will never be lost."

Ultimately, choose your pact based on your curiosity. Remember to let go of previous choices, societal expectations, and top-down assumptions. What excites you? What do you want to learn? Writer Tasshin Fogleman makes the distinction between cold curiosity, which is functional and calculating, and burning curiosity, which is feverish and irrational. Your pact should sit in the in-between: warm curiosity, the kind that both pragmatically aligns with your existing interests and fiercely drives you to explore new ones.

That's it. Beyond choosing a pact in genuine accord with your curiosity, you don't need to have anything else figured out. Each cycle of experimentation will be a chance to discover more about yourself and the world, to expand your skills and your knowledge, and to iterate on your approach based on what you learn.

When you're ready, take a couple of minutes to write down your pact:

I will [action] for [duration].

Congratulations: You have now committed to action instead of stagnation. You have reignited your creative engine with your very first protocol for personal growth. People who complete this exercise during my workshops report feeling confident that they can now move forward. As AI engineer Artur Piszek wrote: "The pact was my favorite [activity] because choosing what to work on is the highest leverage."

By crafting your first pact, you have stepped forward to embrace a life of perpetual transition—not a frightening limbo, but a generative series of experiments.

	LINEAR MINDSET	EXPERIMENTAL MINDSET
RESPONSE TO UNCERTAINTY	**Response 1: Automatic** Fight/Flight/Freeze. Not knowing the destination triggers anxiety.	**Response 2: Autonomous** Engage/Explore/Experiment. Not knowing the destination triggers curiosity.
MENTAL MODEL OF GROWTH	**Ladders** Lists of milestones with predictable outcomes.	**Loops** Cycles of experiments with unpredictable outcomes.
DEFINITION OF SUCCESS	**Outcome-based** Predefined success focused on a fixed destination ("Publish a cookbook by the end of the year").	**Output-based** Emergent success focused on deliberate experimentation ("Write one new recipe every week until the end of the year").
GOAL-SETTING FRAMEWORK	**SMART** Specific Measurable Assignable Realistic Timely	**PACT** Purposeful Actionable Continuous Trackable

No more SMART goal setting; no more five-year career plans; no more life road maps. As long as you complete each trial, success is guaranteed even if you don't know what it looks like—much like Amelia Earhart, who successfully crossed the Atlantic but didn't land at her intended destination.

Many new possibilities will open when you switch from a linear mindset to an experimental mindset and focus on showing up rather than perfecting everything. Whether it's committing to coding every day like Kallaway, publishing one video per week like Abdaal, making twenty paintings like Delgay, or practicing making one full-course dinner for friends every weekend like Loredo, you now have access to the power of experiments rooted in your own curiosity.

ACT

Practice Mindful Productivity

4

⊞ *A Deeper Sense of Time*

Perhaps you are familiar with an arresting, provocative image known as *Your Life in Weeks*. The visualization, popularized by blogger Tim Urban in 2014, is still in wide circulation a decade later. Here it is, in case you missed it:

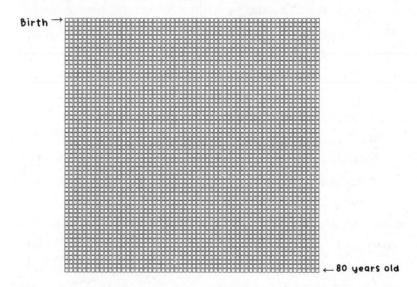

How small and finite life feels when you see it represented like this, as a series of identical squares that can easily fit on a Post-it Note. It's a moving and at times motivating depiction of a hard truth: the number of little boxes given to each of us is limited. The image urgently introduces a question, posed by Urban in his blog, that we all feel like we should be asking ourselves: "Are you making the most of your weeks?"

The trouble is when our productivity-minded culture comes to the rescue with a seemingly obvious solution to answer that question: time management. During the same decade that *Your Life in Weeks* was circulating, and often in the same circles, the obsession with personal productivity skyrocketed. Having combined time scarcity with an efficiency mindset, many people in these circles have developed an anxious urge to pack as much as possible into each remaining box, akin to what Germans call *Torschlusspanik*, the fear of time running out.

When I posted a message asking if any "recovering productivity junkies" would be willing to be interviewed for this book, the responses quickly poured in from around the globe. Unsurprisingly, there were many engineers and startup founders, but the overall group was wildly diverse: an educator from Greece, a nurse from the southern United States, an executive coach from Canada. The efficiency trap, as Oliver Burkeman calls it, doesn't discriminate.

All the people who responded said that focusing on relentless execution had led them to the same place: burnout. There were many varieties of wake-up calls, including disordered sleep, health problems, and even broken relationships. One mentioned "an inability to slow down and enjoy the moment." Another had to relearn that it was okay to walk somewhere even if it took a bit longer than driving. While these answers came from a group of people self-described as "in recovery," burnout is a widely documented ailment of our time. Meanwhile, the desire to make the most of our weeks remains universal. How can we honor this desire without sacrificing our health in the process?

The answer lies in a new way of thinking and doing that can serve as a map to pursue rich, generative lives. But first we need to understand why so many of us see time through the lens of productivity instead of that of curiosity.

In our culture, being a productive member of society is seen as a moral imperative. Management theorist Peter Drucker, considered a founder of modern management theory, wrote in 1999 that the productivity of manual workers had increased fiftyfold over the last century. He concluded: "On this achievement rest all of the economic and social gains of the 20th century." In this environment, it becomes tempting to attach our self-worth to how much we get done. Fundamentally, being productive is a way to say: "I am here, and it makes a difference."

Growing up with role models who highly value productivity—praising grades over effort, obsessing over learning new skills, packing the greatest number of activities into a weekend—can sublimate this outlook as you start attaching a lot of value to productivity yourself. Seeking the approval of parents or professors can turn into seeking the approval of peers through overscheduling, workaholism, and busy bragging—or regularly boasting about one's busyness.

As a result, we treat every square of time as a resource to exploit efficiently. This takes the form of getting the most done in the shortest amount of time, constantly working toward the completion of linear goals. This definition assumes that time is a commodity, which is evident in our language. We *spend* time, *invest* time, *save* time, and *budget* our time. For an activity to be worth our time, it must lead to a tangible outcome. Within that quantitative frame, productivity is seen as a virtue and curiosity as a distraction.

Even if you grew up in an environment that encouraged curiosity, big transitions can be stressful and can cause you to throw yourself into your work as a coping mechanism. The transition might be leveling up through a graduation, a promotion, a shift from management to leadership. Experiencing a major personal change, such as a geographic move, becoming a parent, losing a parent. These are the quintessential liminal moments that might prompt an impetuous desire for control. For instance, a Ness Labs community member told me that his productivity mania emerged when he started a high-stress startup job. He became relentless about logging how he spent every moment, even his extremely limited "leisure time"; if he watched a movie, he put it on a spreadsheet.

Neurodiversity may also be a factor in the obsession with productivity. Some neurodivergent people tend to focus their attention on a narrow range of interests at any time, a behavior known as monotropism in autism and hyperfocus in ADHD. When the topic is productivity, a legitimate interest in how to stay focused and motivated can spiral into a fixation: buying courses, installing applications, and downloading templates— which often paradoxically prove to be distractions from actual work.

"As an autistic person, I have a tendency to get super zoned in and absorbed in things," Martine Ellis, a teacher based in the Channel Islands, told me. "So productivity became a special interest for me, and I needed to know everything about it." Haider Al-Mosawi, who cofounded a startup hub, experienced a similar journey: "I struggled with ADHD, so I ended up spending a lot of time reading books, trying to apply productivity advice." When a simple to-do list wasn't enough, he tried more advanced time-tracking techniques. When these weren't enough, he started designing an ad hoc process. "The burden of the tasks had doubled: on top of doing the things I wanted to do, I also had to optimize my productivity system."

Whatever the trigger, this toxic form of productivity becomes a hidden motive that influences our choices and actions, pushing us toward constant output while downplaying the value of rest, reflection, and meaningful engagement. Each project needs a clear outcome. Conversations become transactional. So-called unproductive moments of playful curiosity and quiet contemplation where our most profound insights can arise are eliminated. There is no space for the mind to wander and make unexpected connections.

Let's be honest: Nobody really wants to live a productive life. We want to express ourselves, connect with others, and explore the world. Productivity is just a means to those ends; it should certainly not come at the expense of actually living life.

Fortunately, while toxic productivity is dangerously seductive, there is a way to recover. It will require you to—at least temporarily—throw out your calendars, your timers, and your to-do lists, and instead embrace a more fulfilling way to orient toward time.

BEYOND TIME MANAGEMENT

The ancient Greeks had not one but two words to speak of time. The first one, *Chronos*, refers to quantity. This is largely how most of us in the modern world relate to time. It is the time of clocks and calendars, of productivity tools and linear goals. The eponymous god is often depicted as a long-bearded old man holding a scythe—a resemblance to the Grim Reaper that is not coincidental. In his poem *Triumph of Time*, Petrarch talks of this implacable marching god:

> *For days and hours and years and months fly on (. . .)*
> *And fleeing thus, it turns the world around.*
> *Nor ever rests nor stays nor turns again*
> *Till it has made you nought but a little dust.*

The blind march of Chronos governs most of our day-to-day existence. Because we treat time as equal, objective units with a finite end, we feel like there's never enough. We are basically all staring at a clock where the inexorable ticking away of time fills us with a sense of urgency and anxiety. Chronos is the time orientation depicted in *Your Life in Weeks*: our weeks, days, or hours as a finite series of identical boxes, each an empty vessel that we can fill with anything. Here today, gone tomorrow.

But those neat boxes are not at all representative of how we experience time. The weeks of our life do not have the same weight. I don't remember the day I was born, but the night before I started school stretched infinitely in my mind. The week I submitted my proposal for this book to publishers felt like an entire month of nervous excitement, doubt, and hope—and had a positive and outsized impact on the years to come. I can remember just about every moment of the day I learned a close friend had passed away, making it seem like that one day lasted for several years.

Think about your own life, trying to remember the weeks that brought you up to this day: Do they all feel identical, like interchangeable units of time? Or does time feel more like a fluid experience?

Deep down, we know this—that time is elastic, that some moments last for what seems like an eternity while others come and go in the blink of an eye. Research into time perception supports that many factors can impact how we process time. Emotional experiences are one such factor: time can seem to expand in moments of acute fear, sadness, or joy, making certain moments feel longer than they objectively are. Are you hungry or tired? Those physiological states can influence your perception of time. Cognitive engagement also plays a significant role. Time drags on forever when you're bored, but it flies by when you're engrossed in a challenging task—a phenomenon related to Mihaly Csikszentmihalyi's concept of flow.

Time also seems to speed up as we become older. Even cultural and social factors can contribute, including the language we use to talk about time. Time, far from being a series of identical and interchangeable units, is a profoundly personal and fluid experience. This is a more accurate representation of *Your Life in Weeks*, as we perceive it:

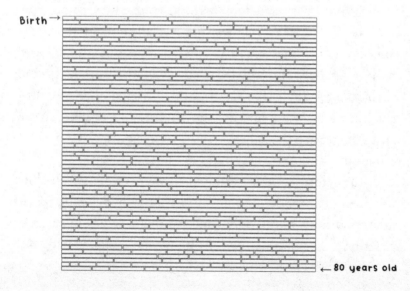

Birth →

← 80 years old

Sure, this depiction looks more chaotic. But there is beauty in this chaos. It means that instead of staring at a gruesome countdown clock, our most expansive, fruitful weeks may yet lie ahead. The shift from a quantitative view of time to a qualitative one is the first huge step toward a healthier approach to getting things done and finding a meaningful answer to how to make the most of our weeks.

The Greeks valued this qualitative view deeply, so much so that they had a second word for time: *Kairos*. Kairos expresses the *quality*, not the *quantity*, of time. It recognizes that each moment is unique, with a unique purpose, rather than a fixed unit to be mechanically allocated. Sometimes the Greeks used the word *Kairos* even more specifically, as an opportune time for action, an opening, the perfect moment.

The region of Brittany in the west of France, where my father was born and I spent most of my summers as a child, is world-renowned for its oyster harvest. Among locals, *pêche à pied*, or on-foot fishing, is a popular pastime. Technically, you can set out any day of the year to gather mussels, oysters, whelks, and other delicious seafood from our shores. However, the wise forager knows that not all moments yield the same bounty. Some shellfish, like razor clams and cockles, can burrow deep into the sediment when the weather is cold, which makes them harder to find. Others, like oysters—which have been dubbed the superheroes of the sea—should not be harvested after heavy rains because they are busy filtering out pollutants, making them unsafe to eat.

Although seafood is available all year round, each fishing expedition is unique, and its success heavily depends on the right conditions at the right time. So the forager understands something that many of us, sitting at our desks, staring at a daily calendar and a clock, lose sight of: not all moments are created equal. Some carry a particular weight, a unique potential; they are the precious ground from which our best ideas and most meaningful experiences can emerge.

Kairos moments, like *pêche à pied,* are what I call magic windows: those periods of creative flow that often occur when we are immersed in activities that capture our full attention, when we spend time with loved ones, or when we are engaged in self-reflection. If you've ever felt like an instant was suspended in time, as if your sphere of consciousness was immune to the world's chaos, you know what I am describing here. Kairos is when you feel like this moment, right now, is perfect.

Kairos captures what the traditional view of productivity ignores—that the value of time depends on the situation. Once-in-a-lifetime opportunities can sometimes feel less important than reading a bedtime story to a child. Spending time alone may become more vital than going out with friends. And of course there are all the unexpected disruptions. A sudden emergency may trump long-planned social events. You may fall sick exactly as you finally manage to find time for a hobby you care about. A trusted collaborator may leave right before a launch, upending your carefully laid plans.

Even in fairly independent careers, our workdays often impose rigid structures, leaving us to navigate the tension between our aspirations and our obligations. "The productivity equation is a nonlinear one," fiction writer Neal Stephenson explains. "If I organize my life in such a way that I get lots of long, consecutive, uninterrupted time-chunks, I can write novels. But as those chunks get separated and fragmented, my productivity as a novelist drops spectacularly."

Within these constraints lies the opportunity to be mindful of our inner states and make the conscious choice to focus on what resonates most at any given time. Embracing Kairos means letting go of the Taylorist ideal* of maximizing every minute and instead appreciating the unique qualities of each moment that make up a life.

To live in Kairos time, we need to shift the focus from *what* we do with our time to *how* we experience each moment—what you might call mindful productivity. It's a simple idea, that making the most of our time isn't about *doing* more but about *being* more: more present, more engaged, and more attuned to the quality of our experiences.

YOUR MAGIC WINDOWS

Although mindfulness and productivity may seem at odds, this is only the case when viewed through a narrow Chronos-based lens. Traditional productivity approaches work from the top down, viewing time as a series of identical boxes into which as much as possible should be crammed.

In contrast to this future-focused, efficiency-driven approach, mindful productivity focuses on the quality of the experience at hand. Employing a bottom-up approach, mindful productivity recognizes the inherent uniqueness of each box and prioritizes the right course of action accordingly.

Time is the most critical resource in traditional productivity. On the other hand, mindful productivity is centered

---

* Frederick Winslow Taylor (1856–1915) was an American mechanical engineer who developed and advocated methods of factory management that included the idea of maximizing every minute.

around managing your physical, cognitive, and emotional resources—the ingredients that give rise to Kairos moments.

PHYSICAL RESOURCES: MANAGING YOUR ENERGY

We have become increasingly reliant on digital timers and time-blocking apps to manage our productivity. Many people use their calendar for micro-scheduling—the practice of breaking each day into small, predefined chunks—and their smartwatch to keep them on track, with reminders right on their wrists. But our most reliable timekeeper might be within us: our internal clock or circadian rhythm. Rather than structuring our work solely around arbitrary schedules, we must consider our natural energy cycles.

Recent genome-wide association studies have identified that our morning or evening preferences, far from being a matter of will, can be traced back to as many as fifteen spots in our genome. You may be a morning lark, a night owl, or what American author Daniel Pink calls a "third bird," where your magic windows fall somewhere in the middle. By understanding your chronotype, you can tune into how your energy levels rise and fall throughout the day in order to determine when you should focus on demanding tasks, when your creativity is at its peak, and when it's best to intentionally pause and recharge.

But it's not just those daily cycles that matter. From monthly hormonal shifts to seasonal changes, numerous natural rhythms can impact your productivity and creativity. For instance, the U.S. women's soccer coaches believe monitoring their players' menstrual cycles was critical to the team's 2019 World Cup victory. The team contracted an expert to provide evidence-based insight at the cutting edge of sports science. Under the guidance of performance coach Dawn Scott and Dr. Georgie Bruinvels, the team's players kept track of their periods and adapted what they ate, when and how long they worked out, and even when they went to sleep based on how much progesterone and estrogen they had in their bodies. The aim was to work *with* their hormones, not against them. During the monthlong World Cup in France, they also had posters in their lodging to remind them of the different stages in their cycle and the changes to make during each one. Instead of a hurdle to overcome, those natural cycles became integral to optimizing their performance. The experience of Rose Lavelle, a midfielder, shows the success of this approach: though she was going through the difficult premenstrual phase on the day of the final, adapting her diet, training load, and sleep schedule helped her perform when it mattered most, scoring the team's second goal in a 2–0 victory.

Whether due to sleep habits, hormonal fluctuations, or seasonal changes, everyone has unique cycles of productivity highs and lows throughout the day, the week, and the year. Researchers found that there may be longer biological rhythms at play, which they call circannual cycles, suggesting that seasons have a complex effect on how the brain works.

Many leaders and creatives throughout the ages have known the value of understanding these daily, weekly, and yearly cycles to work smarter. People as diverse as LeBron James, Arianna Huffington, and Bill Gates are known for prioritizing full nights of sleep. Even Winston Churchill took naps during the day. In his memoir, he wrote: "Nature had not intended mankind to work from eight in the morning until midnight without the refreshment of blessed oblivion which, even if it only lasts 20 minutes, is sufficient to renew all the vital forces." The naturalist Henry David Thoreau, though he recommended that we keep taking nature walks throughout the year, led a more inward life during the winter months. He wrote in his journal: "Live in each season as it passes; breathe the air, drink the drink, taste the fruit, and resign yourself to the influences of each."

Keeping track of your energy levels is an easy way to start managing your physical resources better. For a week or two, make a note of your energy levels at different times of the day so you can identify your energy peaks and troughs. You can add these to your field notes. Or like investor and entrepreneur Sahil Bloom, you can retrospectively color-code your calendar to reflect how different activities affect your energy levels. He uses green for activities that generate energy, yellow for neutral activities, and red for draining ones. Then you can prioritize energy-creating activities and avoid energy-draining ones to maintain a high ratio of green to red.

In addition, consider reevaluating your magic windows to keep them in sync with your energy levels. Many believe they are morning larks or night owls but haven't reassessed this in years. As you grow older, changes in your lifestyle and responsibilities can influence your natural rhythms. For instance, young adults may find themselves more alert in the evening hours, but as they age find their best hours are in the morning. It's worth setting aside preconceived notions and, if you can, experimenting with different working hours, observing when you feel most alert for a few weeks. This process can bring surprising insights and unveil new magic windows in previously overlooked parts of your day.

Finally, heed and honor your body's signals. Yawning frequently or feeling mentally foggy are cues from your body that you need a rest. Instead of pushing through with caffeine or other stimulants, take a power nap or a short break.

The change you should aim for might look like this in practice. Imagine coming back from a busy and hypersocial travel weekend. The efficiency mindset encourages you to dive headfirst into your work on Monday. You'd set your alarm for half an hour earlier, arrive at your desk on time, and immediately tackle the most daunting tasks, your heart racing from the coffee rush that helps you stay awake through countless meetings.

The mindful productivity approach offers a kinder path. Recognizing that you have little energy after an intense weekend, you get all your easier administrative work for the week done on Monday. You also shift some meetings to Tuesday so you can fit in twenty minutes of meditation or movement in the morning to recharge—or sleep an extra twenty minutes. Your big tasks for that week still get done, but you don't endure any unnecessary strain.

Managing your physical resources ultimately boils down to discarding the unrealistic expectation of always being "at your best." Energy naturally fluctuates; attempting to maintain a perpetual peak is not just impossible but detrimental to your well-being. Respecting your natural rhythms can lead you to have a healthier relationship to work as well as increased productivity and creativity.

COGNITIVE RESOURCES: MANAGING YOUR EXECUTIVE FUNCTION

Once you've identified your magic windows, you're faced with a crucial question: What belongs there? It would be great if you could tackle everything that matters to you at once, but while the human mind is extraordinary, its cognitive capabilities are not limitless—yet. We are constrained by what cognitive scientists call executive function, which is our ability to successfully select and monitor our actions.

We fancy ourselves adept multitaskers, but studies show that our performance drops dramatically when we attempt to focus on more than one thing at a time. That's because the human brain has an attentional bottleneck impacting both perception and action. In short, our efforts to get more done actually slow us down.

Working memory also limits how much you can achieve during your magic windows. You can think of working memory as the mental workspace where you process and manipulate information. Using your working memory is akin to juggling several pieces of information, holding them in mind while you make decisions, solve problems, and have conversations. There's a limit to how many balls you can keep in the air at once. As Dr. Bill Cerbin, professor emeritus of psychology and director of the Center for Advancing Teaching and Learning at the University of Wisconsin–La Crosse, says, "Humans are endowed with remarkable cognitive capacities, but one area where we are seriously limited is working memory."

How can you manage these cognitive bottlenecks? The key is to use sequential focus—doing one thing at a time—by accepting that you can't maintain equal effort across all the essential aspects of your life, deciding moment to moment what your priority is (your family, work, or yourself) and giving that your undivided attention. There will always be competing priorities. Instead of trying to maintain an artificial balance—to keep all the balls in the air simultaneously—you can use sequential focus to choose one priority at a time and devote all your energy to it.

Sequential focus isn't the same as time-blocking, where

you segment your day in advance with predefined tasks. Rather, sequential focus leans into the ebb and flow of your cognitive capacity, prompting you to evaluate constantly: *Given my current attention and working memory, what is the most sensible task to undertake right now?*

Consider the environment around you. If you're at home and your kids are within earshot, you might want to reserve this time for lighter tasks that don't demand your undivided focus. On the other hand, if you have a couple of hours of uninterrupted time and an upcoming presentation dominates your thoughts, you might dive into that.

Account for your mental state. Maybe recent criticism has been weighing heavily on your mind. When this happens, confront those distracting thoughts straight on. Sit down, reflect on that feedback, and write down your thoughts on paper or in a note-taking app. Then, go back to your task—those reflections will be there to go back to when you are ready.

Above all, avoid the allure of multitasking. It might feel productive, but dividing your focus is a surefire way to lower the quality of your work. Focus your entire attention on one activity. Close all other apps, leave your phone in another room, and make sure people around you know that you are in focus mode—for example, by closing the door or wearing your headphones.

EMOTIONAL RESOURCES: MANAGING YOUR EMOTIONS

Madonna, who has released fourteen studio albums, said that there was a time when she would cry from exhaustion before about half of the shows during one of her tours, but she would still press on. "There's no such thing as not in the mood because the show must go on," she stated. Like Madonna, we can be very successful by obsessively pushing ourselves to work nonstop, but the constant strain will still affect our mental health. If we press on for too long, we might even reach a point of no return, unable to keep the show on the road. And, unlike Madonna, we may not have the ability to take ourselves on a multimillion-dollar retreat.

Stress isn't always bad for us. In fact, a certain degree of stress—known as eustress, which means "good stress" in Greek—can boost performance. But like a sandpile growing increasingly unstable with each grain added, our stress levels can accrue until the slightest increment triggers an avalanche. This mental avalanche isn't a sudden occurrence but the culmination of accumulated stressors that have hit a critical point. It's crucial, then, that we understand when eustress is tipping over into distress.

However, we have become terrible at listening to ourselves. We know we should stay connected to our inner states and take care of our well-being, yet we struggle to put these ideas into practice. To fulfill our responsibilities, we overlook the vital signals our emotions are trying to relay. It may be hard to fall asleep at night. Maybe we're easily irritated. We feel anxious for no apparent reason, a phenomenon psychologists refer to as free-floating anxiety. Something feels off, and yet we power through.

It's the equivalent of a store owner who, facing an ever-growing line of customers, starts operating mechanically to keep up with the demand, processing transactions quickly but without the attentiveness that once defined the company's service. The owner, though physically present, is emotionally disengaged. It may feel productive, but this robotic approach soon leads to a decline in the quality of customer interactions.

Instead of trying to endure those symptoms by directing

your attention elsewhere, hit pause to reconnect with how you feel on the inside. One of the simplest strategies to regulate your emotions is to stimulate your body's parasympathetic nervous system, which acts like a brake on the stress response. All you need to do is move your body. Moving your body has been found to relieve anxiety straightaway and to create a virtuous cycle that reduces anxiety over the long term. And it's completely free.

It doesn't need to be a full-on stretching session. You don't even have to get up if you can't. You just need a few fluid movements. You could slowly roll your shoulders up and down or subtly shift your weight from side to side while standing, stretching the muscles in your legs and hips. Even small movements such as rotating your wrists or ankles can stimulate your parasympathetic nervous system. Pay attention to the sensations in your stomach, your lungs, your heart. What's important is to focus on the inner experience of the movement instead of what it looks like from the outside.

Noticing your emotions and regulating your nervous system will help you develop what Susan David calls emotional agility, the ability to fluidly adapt and respond to your emotional experiences. When emotionally agile, you can navigate your emotional landscape effectively and prevent certain psychophysiological responses such as free-floating anxiety from holding you captive. You will be able to do your best work without sacrificing your well-being.

YOUR ENERGY, EXECUTIVE function, and emotions are the three pillars of a fulfilling life—a life in which contributing to the wider world doesn't come at the expense of your inner world. In summary, mindful productivity aims to answer three questions:

- **Managing your energy:** When is my magic window?

- **Managing your executive function:** What belongs in this window?

- **Managing your emotions:** How can I keep the window open?

To manage your physical resources, use energy syncing to align your most demanding tasks with your daily energy peaks and block a weekly magic window for strategic work. For your cognitive resources, apply sequential focus to tackle one major task at a time, considering how your environment impacts your attention and off-loading worries to your notes so you can free up some working memory. For your emotional resources, practice conscious movement whenever you notice any signals of distress.

DOMAIN	PRINCIPLE	PRACTICE
Physical	Energy: Align tasks with natural rhythms.	Energy syncing
Cognitive	Executive function: Avoid multitasking.	Sequential focus
Emotional	Emotions: Adapt stress response.	Conscious movement

Unfortunately, you will find that our society still frequently requires you to conform to a Chronos worldview. Unless you live on a desert island with no responsibilities, you can't always allow your inner states to guide your outward actions. We have appointments, deadlines, and other time-bound obligations. We make plans with friends but sometimes wish we were doing something else when the moment arrives. Our jobs may occasionally require us to work late into the night. In short, life is going to happen.

So how can we return ourselves to the presence of Kairos when Chronos seems to be in control? How can we shift into a state of *being* when *doing* is compulsory?

DESIGNING A KAIROS RITUAL

What do walking in a slow circle, making a cup of tea, and listening to a favorite playlist have in common? They're all ways people I know ground themselves so they can do their best work.

I call these Kairos rituals. These small acts help you open a magic window for something you want to direct all your resources toward, whatever might be going on in the larger scope of your life. It's a practice to call forth your highest sense of awareness.

While meditating or doing yoga can be excellent vectors for expanded awareness, they can be difficult to sustain when life is at its busiest. Fortunately, they're not the only ways to stay in touch with our inner self. Being mindful means interrupting the autopilot mode we often use on a day-to-day basis, taking the time to appreciate the little things, and observing how we feel at a physical, cognitive, and emotional level. As such, a Kairos ritual is a way to see the present moment clearly. Here are some Kairos rituals in the wild:

"I look for a corner of the room and I sit on the floor. It's cozy and gives a different perspective on my surroundings. Then I switch on my meditation app and do a quick breathing exercise."
—*Agathe Cury, video editor*

"I stretch my body while walking slowly in a circle in the room. And if I'm at home, I will go lie down on my bed for just a few minutes and then get back to work."
—*François Singer, partnerships manager in the sports industry*

"I listen to the kind of music that puts me in a good mood and bob my head along to the beat."
—*Anaïs Ait Ouazzou, account manager at a startup*

"I go to another room, close the door, and take a few deep breaths. Closing the door creates the sense of a separate space." —*Manuela Da Cunha, nurse*

"I head to the kitchen and make myself a cup of tea. The process takes five minutes and allows me to disconnect long enough to head back with renewed calm."
—*Jem Chevillotte, film director*

Kairos rituals are as idiosyncratic as the people who practice them. As you develop your own, think about a simple action that can quickly shift your mood, such as music or scent; reconnect you to your body, such as stretching or conscious breathing; or give you the chance to check in with yourself, such as making a handwritten list of your intentions for the rest of your workday.

These rituals are powerful because of their simplicity, not despite it. They easily become habitual because they integrate so seamlessly into the rhythms of everyday life and the fabric of your workday. It is the accessibility of Kairos rituals— their gentle yet persistent nudge pulling us back to the present—that gives them the transformative power to open magic windows at will.

Physically, they guide you to pause and recalibrate your energy levels. Cognitively, they interrupt your autopilot mode, allowing you to recenter your focus and approach tasks with renewed clarity. Emotionally, these rituals offer a sanctuary— a momentary retreat to acknowledge your feelings, validate your experiences, and reconnect with your inner self. Kairos rituals function as mini resets, priming you for action and ensuring that all your faculties operate in synergy.

There are two key factors in choosing a Kairos ritual. The first is practicality. You may not be able to get up and dance or light candles in the office. Choose a ritual that you can easily use whenever you need to reconnect with yourself and with the present moment, even if it's just mindfully sipping tea, jotting down one thing you're grateful for on a sticky note, or gazing at a photo that brings you a sense of calm. The second, most importantly, is to select a ritual that resonates with you personally. It should be something you look forward to and enjoy, not something that feels like a chore.

Now, whenever you need to anchor yourself in the present moment, you can use that ritual to switch to a Kairos-based mode of being, synced with your energy levels, leveraging your executive function, and connected with your emotions.

Mindful productivity provides you with the necessary scaffolding to fulfill your pact and live a life of curiosity. When you focus on *being* more—finding ways to be present and to slow down time—you can avoid burnout without abandoning your ambitions.

✷ *Procrastination Is Not the Enemy*

Procrastination may feel like a puzzle, especially when what you are procrastinating on is the pact or another activity you have willingly chosen and designed for yourself. But instead of helping you *solve* the puzzle, the internet is teeming with resources to *beat* procrastination.

Many popular remedies are based on self-discipline. A close friend of mine once used the term *white-knuckling*—you clench really hard and hope that your willpower will prevail. Others recommend bullying yourself into doing the "right" thing—for example, by attaching punishment to the noncompletion of a task. There's the Ulysses technique—just as in the scene from Homer's *Odyssey*, you tie yourself up so you have no choice in the matter and can therefore resist the sirens of distraction. Victor Hugo asked his staff to hide his clothes so he could not leave the house until he was done writing for the day. The founder of an online community for entrepreneurs told me he committed to donating money to a political party he loathed if he didn't do what he set out to do. You can even buy the equivalent of digital rope: today, startups sell boxes with a lock so you can put your phone away while working.

Even the more reasonable advice out there is still designed to help you barrel through that nasty procrastination and get back to work: block time in your schedule, break it into smaller steps and set a timer, or find an accountability partner—anything to put the genie back into the lamp and feel in control. But as you well know, these strategies rarely pan out in the long run. You schedule time, but then don't bother to check your calendar; you set a timer on your phone, then ignore it; you stop meeting with your accountability partner—at first pretending you had an emergency and then slowly letting it slide.

There is a reason why none of these methods work, and it has nothing to do with laziness or lack of discipline. They fall short because they rest on a reductive reading of why we procrastinate.

DEATH BY TWO ARROWS

"Such a good morning's writing I'd planned, and wasted the cream of my brain on the telephone," the author Virginia Woolf wrote in her diary in 1920. And more than two thousand years ago, the ancient Greek poet Hesiod wrote: "Do not put your work off till tomorrow and the day after; for a sluggish worker does not fill his barn, nor one who puts off his work: industry makes work go well, but a man who puts off work is always at hand-grips with ruin."

The words *wasted* and *ruin* encapsulate how we have perceived procrastination for millennia. Procrastination is a character flaw that goes against our society's prized virtues of diligence and responsibility, an undesirable trait that casts doubt on your reliability and commitment. When it comes to productivity, procrastination is Public Enemy No. 1. This negative attitude about procrastination is self-defeating and makes it unnecessarily stress-inducing.

As in the teachings of the Buddha, there are two arrows. The first arrow that strikes is procrastination itself, in the form of myriad activities we can turn to while avoiding our tasks—scrolling instead of studying, watching TV instead of working, browsing shopping sites instead of writing. Procrastination might not be new, but the number and attractiveness of distractions available today are like an army of sirens, amplified and autotuned. The problem, however, runs deeper than a craving to binge on that latest award-winning TV show.

That first arrow you could survive; it's the second arrow that's the real killer. That arrow is not the procrastination itself; it's your emotional reaction to it. Studies have found that adverse psychological reactions such as anxiety and shame often accompany procrastination. No surprise, given that we have been taught to equate procrastination with being worthless. "There is nothing like the downward spiral of procrastination to make you feel like an abject failure," said Dr. Tim Pychyl, one of the world's foremost experts on procrastination. "That's why the strongest emotion associated with procrastination is guilt."

So although we want more than anything to put procrastination behind us, we are in the worst possible psychological state to do so. Instead of calm and confident, we feel deeply frustrated, at war with our very sense of self. What if we replaced that second arrow with curiosity instead?

Changing your relationship with procrastination starts with a more accurate understanding of its true nature. Thanks to scientific research, we now know that procrastination is not a moral failure; it's a listening failure. And this is why trying to "beat" procrastination is worse than ineffective. It's counterproductive.

Imagine your brain as a team that works together to make decisions and get things done, with some tasks requiring more teamwork than others. The limbic system and the fronto-parietal network are two key players on this team. The limbic system, a network of brain structures such as the amygdala and the hippocampus, is the passionate team member, playing a key role in our emotional responses and interacting with other brain areas for complex emotional processing. It's one of the brain's oldest and most dominant portions, and its processes are mostly automatic. It can drive us to act based on the desire for immediate satisfaction or protection. Then we have the frontoparietal network, the strategic and meticulous team member that helps us focus, solve problems, make complex decisions, and plan ahead.

Researchers looked at the white matter of the brains of more than nine hundred people and found that procrastination is linked to specific patterns of brain connectivity. One of them is a weakened connection between the limbic system and the frontoparietal network. So while procrastination is often portrayed as a battle between the present self and the future self, involving calculations of the cost and reward of doing something now versus doing it later, it should really be described as poor teamwork between our emotional and our rational selves.

A lot of the pain we experience when we procrastinate stems from viewing it as an enemy to fight against and overcome, instead of a partner to understand and collaborate with. The problem with procrastination is not that you've been lazy. The problem is that you shot the messenger.

Let's see what happens when we take a different approach— slowing down to listen to the signals from all team members in our brain and encouraging them to work together.

DON'T SHOOT THE MESSENGER

Ironically, it took me a long time to start writing this chapter. Instead, I finished writing a grant proposal, cleaned up my notes, learned how to use a new AI transcription tool, and even created little avatars for my team members so we can use them in public materials. It was one of the most productive weeks of the year so far. The only thing I didn't do was what I was actually supposed to do: draft this chapter.

Just like advising a friend who is feeling down to "just cheer up," telling yourself to "just do it" when you procrastinate is not going to get you anywhere. When you try to repress the source of that awful feeling, you deprive yourself of valuable information. You are essentially wandering in the dark, stuck in a cycle of inaction and frustration.

After a few days of circling around my avoidance when trying to work on this chapter, I finally decided to stop ignoring the signals procrastination was trying to send me. The tension I was experiencing was puzzling. Over the years, I had extensively read and written about procrastination, and I thought this chapter would be a breeze to write. And yet somehow I was struggling. What was going on?

I pulled my field notes and started actively capturing observations about my responses whenever I opened the document. Some behavioral patterns started emerging. As soon as I sat down to review research papers, I would check my emails to see if anything else needed my attention. Then I would go through my to-do list to find a more urgent task—anything to feel like I was too busy to work on this chapter.

Digging deeper, I realized that this avoidance stemmed from a feeling of inadequacy. How could I write about a challenge I was still often experiencing myself? Furthermore, I felt a sense of incompleteness in relying solely on research papers after having had so many rich and nuanced conversations about procrastination over the years. Synthesizing the research literature—the academic approach I had been trained in—would not cut it. I needed to talk to people.

I stopped reading papers and started conducting interviews to collect real-life stories of procrastination. I asked: What does it feel like when you procrastinate? What is your instinctive response?

When I stopped trying to shoot the messenger—to "just do it" and plow through—then procrastination turned out to be a helpful friend. When I treated resistance as evidence, it helped me to understand why it was so hard to write this chapter in the first place. And once I started talking to people, it became impossible to keep on delaying the work. I left each conversation energized and eager to learn more. The real-world insights I collected became fuel for questions I could explore further with research. Beyond this specific chapter, understanding the source of my resistance completely reshaped my approach to writing this book. Instead of using only scientific studies, I would also collect stories and harness the collective intelligence of my community.

Just as I explored the source of my resistance instead of recoiling from it, you can examine your procrastination with kindness and curiosity. Are you suddenly feeling tired whenever you try to get started with a specific task? Do you avoid working on a project by reading about the tools you may need further down the line? Do you block time in your calendar only to then ignore your scheduled work sessions?

If you choose to ask these questions in a nonjudgmental way and interpret the answer constructively, procrastination can be a helpful indicator, shifting your internal monologue from self-blame to self-discovery.

Maybe you're putting off writing a report because you're concerned it won't be perfect. Maybe you're avoiding a project because you don't know where to start or because it doesn't excite you. Or maybe the task is designed in a way that makes it unnecessarily overwhelming.

Rather than being an indication of laziness or lack of discipline, procrastination points to nuanced psychological roadblocks that need addressing.

THE TRIPLE CHECK

If you go back to its most basic definition, procrastination means not doing what you think you should be doing. As we have seen, it's not a neutral experience: because we blame ourselves for acting against our better judgment, procrastination is usually accompanied by feelings of shame and guilt.

Those feelings are caused by the word *should* towering over you like a dictator demanding that you fulfill your duty. As philosopher Susanna Newsonen puts it: "Should is a shame-based statement that creates stress and anxiety in your body and mind." The unresolved conflict between expectations and actions—between an idealized vision of yourself and the current reality of your behavior—leads to emotional distress and decreased self-esteem.

When we procrastinate, we remain stuck at that first-order level of analysis: we should be doing something, but we're not. We chalk up this contradictory behavior to a fatal defect in our character. In contrast to this sterile self-judgment, we might instead ask ourselves a potentially fertile question:

Why are you procrastinating?

Answering this question is a bit like playing a game of Clue (or Cluedo, outside of the United States), where the objective is to deduce the details of a crime. With six characters, six weapons, and nine rooms, Clue offers hundreds of permutations. Fortunately, the list of possible explanations for your procrastination is much shorter. In fact, the many reasons why you may be procrastinating can be divided into just three categories: they can stem from your head, your heart, or your hand.

This division originated in the mind of Johann Heinrich Pestalozzi, born in 1746 in Zürich. Pestalozzi was supposed to become a clergyman. But when he read the work of philosopher Jean-Jacques Rousseau, it forever changed his career path. Convinced that education should be available to all, regardless of their social or economic standing, he made it his mission to promote inclusive education in Switzerland. This was a radical idea at the time, as education was often reserved for the wealthy. Pestalozzi summarized his belief in holistic education with a motto: "Learning by head, hand, and heart."

Centuries later, in the late 1990s, Professor Hugo M. Kehr would adopt this motto for his research in motivational psychology. Then a young scholar, he moved from Germany to California, bringing six boxes full of research papers in the hold of the plane thanks to "a special arrangement with the airline," as he told me. After delving into the scientific literature on what motivates people to work, he found that most theories were from the 1960s and no longer relevant. He decided to look into developing a new model. At the University of California, Berkeley, he tirelessly devoted six to eight hours daily to reading, writing, and refining his research, until he finally settled on a three-factor model. The model is advanced in its thinking but elegant in its execution, illustrating how human motivation arises from the interplay of rational (head), affectional (heart), and practical (hand) factors.

Rational factors include explicit motives. It's your head telling you what it thinks is the right thing to do. The affectional factors are your implicit motives. It's your heart telling you what would feel good or not so good to do. Finally, the practical factors pertain to your perceived abilities—the skills, knowledge, and tools you believe you'll need to perform the action. It's your hand telling you what it believes it can do.

The work of Professor Kehr focuses on theories of motivation and doesn't specifically mention procrastination, but it takes only a few tweaks to adapt it for the purpose of our detective work. Whenever you're procrastinating, ask yourself whether it's coming from the head, the heart, or the hand:

- **Head:** "Is the task appropriate?"

- **Heart:** "Is the task exciting?"

- **Hand:** "Is the task doable?"

When you have been putting things off for a little while, you can perform a quick mental check to answer these questions. For longer bouts of procrastination, I like to pull out my journal or open my note-taking app and write it down. Writing helps me untangle the different factors of procrastination and dig deeper into why this is happening. I call this process the Triple Check.

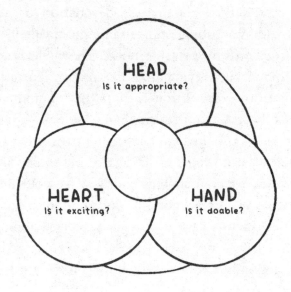

HEAD

Let's look at the first question: "Is the task appropriate?" You want to determine whether this course of action is the wisest. If the answer is no or unclear, this means you are skeptical about the potential benefits of the task. For small tasks with no dependencies—in other words, tasks not connected to other tasks—remove them from your to-do list. It's one of the simplest ways to save your valuable energy.

For more substantial tasks, you will need to dig deeper. Let's say that you're putting off recording a YouTube video.

In such cases, write down why you don't think this task is the right approach. Is the topic inconsistent with your YouTube channel's theme? Is it popular but not intellectually stimulating to you? Have recent industry events rendered your planned content irrelevant? After identifying the reasons, reconsider your strategy to ensure the task aligns with your current priorities and the impact you wish to have.

James Clear, author of the bestselling book *Atomic Habits,* provides a good illustration of this scenario. The habit that launched his career was writing a new article on Mondays and Thursdays, which he did for three years. But after his book came out, he started feeling resistance when he was writing the biweekly newsletter. After giving it some thought, he decided that sending a regular newsletter was still crucial but that his strategy had to change. Instead of simply scaling back or watering down his previous format, he took the time to genuinely explore potential alternatives.

"After the book came out, I tried to step back and realized that I needed a different style of newsletter," he told me. "I pondered if there was a version I could create in just one or two hours a week that wouldn't just match the quality of what I was doing but would actually be better. I believed that among the myriad of possibilities, there had to be something superior to my current approach that still fit within my time constraint." This process of deliberate reflection resulted in the creation of his 3-2-1 newsletter—three ideas from James, two quotes from others, and one question for the reader to ponder—a much shorter format that has now amassed millions of readers.

You may not always be able to make the final call on how to proceed with a project. Some people might be expecting a specific pre-agreed output from you, and you must consult them before changing the strategy. Understanding why you have reservations is still the first step in such circumstances. Only then can you raise these concerns with your team, clients, or other stakeholders. Addressing the disconnect you noticed between the objective and the task is essential to engaging in constructive conversations and rethinking the strategy together. This process may require some tough discussions, but it will be harder in the long run if you don't treat procrastination as a helpful signal that should be taken seriously and acted upon.

HEART

If you think the strategy is sound on paper, the problem may come from your subconscious feelings. Simply asking yourself, *Is the task exciting?* is a great prompt to identify what you're feeling. Open your field notes and write down your response. The lack of excitement might be due to fear, boredom, or irritation—or perhaps the task simply doesn't align with your personal definition of fun. Since it feels tedious, you procrastinate—even though you've established at a rational level (in your head) that you want to do the task.

In many cases, our feelings become clear quickly, and merely identifying them is enough to get us unstuck. This is a process called affective labeling, which we will explore further in chapter 9.

If the problem runs deeper, you may need a more introspective approach. Set a timer for ten minutes and free-write about the task. Let your feelings flow without judgment or editing. Then review what you've written for patterns. For example, do you notice a rise in negative feelings when the task involves a certain person, situation, or topic? Is the anxiety you are experiencing linked to a past event? Perhaps perfectionism is causing fear of failure. Do you have some history with the task that is weighing you down?

The stronger the feelings, the more tempting it can be to shut them down—and the more important it is to lean into those feelings with curiosity instead of self-blame. "There is something emotional and somatic around big work projects," Nibras Ib, a product designer and strategist, told me. "Nowadays I watch the avoidance start to play out. I've tried to sit and open my laptop seven times, and every time I find myself across the room. If it was a child doing this, I wouldn't beat and berate them. Instead, I'd observe them and ask: What are they doing? At what moment do they get up and leave their laptop? What do they do after getting up?"

After completing this exercise a few times, you will become better at identifying where your heart is influencing your behavior. For instance, I used to put off preparing presentation materials until the last minute. After journaling several times about it, I now know that my fear of public speaking is lurking behind that procrastination. Nowadays I can skip the journaling and give myself a little pep talk or practice conscious movement, which helps me proceed with the work.

For feelings that elicit stronger resistance, you can use what behavioral scientists call a pairing method to help you get started. If the task is sound but feels dreary, pair it with an enjoyable activity. You can catch up on overdue emails from your favorite coffee shop, do your taxes while listening to your favorite band, or turn the task into a game by creating rewards for each completed chunk. If the task feels daunting, you can ask a friend to cowork with you to catch up and boost your confidence.

HAND

The last question, "Is the task doable?," may seem to be the simplest one to solve for. You might have existing skills from other projects that are transferable to this new challenge. And if you don't believe the task is doable with your current knowledge and tools, then you can address the problem by obtaining these resources. Start by asking around if a friend, a fellow student, or someone on your team could help you with the task—in a way, asking if they can give you a hand. If not, consider taking an online course or finding a coach.

A note of caution: It's important to notice when we use learning as procrastination in disguise. Sometimes what we think is a lack of skills really is a lack of self-assurance. Reading books or listening to podcasts on the subject won't help until you apply the knowledge to the task you have been putting off. That's why getting input from a more experienced person is often the best way to go. They will narrow down the scope of what you need to learn and may even point out that you already know enough to get started.

SOURCE	EXPLANATION	SOLUTION
Head	I don't think the task is appropriate.	Redefine strategy
Heart	I don't feel like the task is exciting.	Redesign the experience
Hand	I don't believe the task is doable.	Request support or get training

Identifying the source of your procrastination will help make the shift from self-blame to self-discovery by providing both an explanation and a practical solution. Is the task appropriate, exciting, and doable? When the answer to all three questions is yes, then your head, your heart, and your hand are in harmony. I like to call this harmonious state *aligned aliveness*. Not only is it easy to get started, but it is also much easier to keep going.

If you are missing one or more of those components, you will find yourself fighting an internal battle and trying to rely on willpower to accomplish a task—a war you will inevitably lose.

As soon as you become aware of a discrepancy between your head, your heart, and your hand, take this as a signal to reconsider your approach.

LOOKING OUTSIDE YOURSELF

What happens when your head, heart, and hand are perfectly aligned, and *still* you find yourself procrastinating? It might be time to consider whether the problem lies not within you but within the system in which you operate.

Amy, a registered nurse in North Carolina, responded to one of my public calls to discuss these subjects. Being a nurse wasn't just a profession to her, but a meaningful act of service that made a real difference in people's lives. She had a genuine interest in her patients' well-being and loved taking care of them. She even received her master's degree as a working mother because she wanted to keep on expanding her skills.

But even nurses find moments to procrastinate. "I would often find myself thinking, *I've got to go give this one o'clock med*." But instead of staying on schedule, she'd continue chatting with fellow nurses, taking a few moments to relax. It sounds innocent enough, but it was tough for Amy to tell me about it, because the behavior was so at odds with her commitment to patient care. It made her feel ashamed, but she still did it sometimes. Always, she blamed herself.

Amy never stopped to think that she might have a justifiable reason for stealing away a few moments of peace whenever she could. Over the years she spent in the field, the number of patients a single nurse was expected to cover—the very definition of productivity in a hospital setting—went higher and higher. Then came the pandemic, and the hospitals were flooded with patients in urgent need. A short time to gossip and chat with colleagues was her only chance to regain her equilibrium in a high-stress environment. In a system that left nurses in a near-constant state of overwhelm, procrastination wasn't a sign of personal inefficiency but rather a vital act of self-preservation.

It was only after losing a patient during the pandemic, a loss that was partly due to being stretched too thin, that Amy and others began to think: *This isn't a personal failure, it's a systemic failure.* Even before patient counts rose, the workplace culture had already celebrated nurses who pushed themselves to the brink with more responsibilities and longer hours. Amy often volunteered to cover weekends and overnight shifts. Taking time off was frowned upon. The system was designed to relentlessly extract every ounce of energy from its nurses; meanwhile, the ever-increasing productivity demands ensured that their efforts were never quite enough.

Amy reevaluated how the system impacted her mental health and quit her hospital job for an administrative position. By the time she left, she had accumulated three hundred hours of unused paid time off. She said the reason she was willing to be so candid with me, despite how uncomfortable it made her, was that she felt it was essential to be honest about the realities she faced in the hopes of prompting a much-needed discussion—and ultimately, a systemic change.

Because procrastination has so long been considered a moral failure, it's easy to internalize the challenges it brings. But if your head, heart, and hand are aligned and you are still stuck, look outside yourself for answers. Once you recognize the systemic barriers, you can seek support from colleagues, supervisors, or professional networks to advocate for changes. Alternatively, you can decide to prioritize your mental health and exit the system, as Amy did. This, too, is a valid choice, ensuring that your head, heart, and hand are aligned in other meaningful ways.

A DOOR TO DISCOVERY

Sometimes procrastination can help reveal our innate curiosities. In addition to diagnosing why you are procrastinating—head, heart, or hand—you can take a moment to consider what you often find yourself doing when putting things off. Are you reading about a particular topic, exploring a hobby, or like Amy, connecting with other people?

These may seem like idle diversions, but they could tell you something important about yourself, pointing you to an exciting path that could be beneficial to explore. Maybe it's even time for a new pact.

Constantly watching home improvement videos while avoiding other tasks may suggest a latent interest in exploring interior design. If you often turn to cooking when procrastination strikes, consider devoting more time to learning about the culinary arts. These activities we turn to aren't just distractions; they're often expressions of our genuine interests.

As you become adept at hearing its message, procrastination ceases to be a barrier to productivity and becomes a gateway to self-discovery.

6

The Power of Intentional
Imperfection

Shonda Rhimes's career can only be described as a resounding success. Just a few years after graduating, she had worked
on a documentary that won a Peabody Award, made a short
film starring Jada Pinkett Smith, wrote the script for Brit-
ney Spears's debut film, and collaborated on a Disney movie
with one of her idols, British actor Julie Andrews. When
she was asked to create a new pilot for ABC, she decided she
would coproduce the show so she could have a say beyond
scriptwriting. The show—one of the few to use a color-blind
casting technique and one of the longest-running scripted
prime-time television series in the United States—was *Grey's
Anatomy*.

As a lead writer and coproducer, Rhimes could have continued to develop shows for ABC. And she did, for a while.
You may know her from *Scandal* and *How to Get Away
with Murder*. But soon enough, she yearned to explore new
playgrounds. She launched an online magazine and podcasting company to explore different modes of communication.

Then she joined Netflix, which offered her more creative freedom. Her latest production, *Bridgerton,* made history as one of the very few Netflix shows with over 500 million views in the first twenty-eight days.

How does she do it all?

In a commencement speech she delivered at Dartmouth College, Rhimes said: "The answer is this: I don't. Whenever you see me somewhere succeeding in one area of my life, that almost certainly means that I am failing in another area of my life." She might neglect a script rewrite because she is sewing her kids' Halloween costumes. She might miss bath and story time at home because she is focused on finishing a script at work. She might not be there for Sandra Oh's last scene ever being filmed for *Grey's Anatomy* because she's attending her daughter's debut in her school musical. "If I am excelling at one thing, something else is falling off. And that is completely okay," she said in an interview with *Time* magazine.

Rhimes has achieved remarkable success not by striving for unattainable perfection but by embracing the perpetual juggle of life, where we must stay in movement—never quite achieving balance but constantly directing our attention to what is most important in the here and now. In the previous chapter, you learned how to lean into procrastination. Now let's learn how to lean into imperfection.

THE PRESSURE TO BE PERFECT

Perfectionism comes in many shapes and sizes: being afraid of making mistakes, setting sky-high standards, constantly feeling the weight of others' expectations, or overanalyzing our every move. This unhealthy pursuit of perfection doesn't emerge in a vacuum. It's rooted in our past experiences, family dynamics, and beliefs about ourselves.

Perhaps as a child, you were surrounded by critical parents or caregivers with rigid high expectations. Perhaps you mostly received praise based on your achievements and never for your effort or progress. Or perhaps you strived to be perfect as a way to create some sense of safety in a chaotic home.

These experiences can lead us to tie our self-esteem to our accomplishments. When love, acceptance, and attention seem conditional on our achievements, it creates a deep-seated sense of inadequacy that makes us feel that we're never quite good enough. We tirelessly strive toward unattainable perfection, which not only stifles our curiosity but inevitably leads to disappointment when we fall short of our own unrealistic expectations. Self-criticism becomes the default response to perceived failure.

But failure is an integral part of growth, and embracing imperfection is necessary to live a life of creative adventure. As theoretical physicist Stephen Hawking once said: "One of the basic rules of the universe is that nothing is perfect. Perfection simply doesn't exist. Without imperfection, neither you nor I would exist." Fortunately, we can adopt a more compassionate approach to life—one that celebrates our efforts and embraces intentional imperfection rather than striving for impossible perfection.

SWEET AND SOUR

When philosopher Gloria Origgi and sociology professor Diego Gambetta of Oxford University first met, they bonded over memories of their native Italy, noticing the differences between their experience of working and studying overseas and the way things were done back home. They exchanged stories about showing up at Italian conferences only to find their allotted speaking time had been cut in half or doubled, the number of attendees they were told to expect was wrong, or their proofs had not been amended, among other chaotic occurrences.

This conversation prompted them to collaborate on research into why we settle for mediocrity. In a joint theoretical paper, they asked themselves: "How is this unpleasant feeling that nothing works well and standards in many walks of life keep declining compatible with a common appreciation of the Italian laid-back way of life?"

Italy is renowned for its culinary heritage, rich history, and breathtaking natural scenery, but perhaps most of all, for its incarnation of the *dolce vita*—"the sweet life." This cultural tenet is a testament to Italians' capacity to savor life's simplest joys, from leisurely strolls to intimate chats. Life is designed around embracing the beauty in simplicity, taking time to live, and relishing every bit of it. But there is a sour side to the dolce vita. As one of my friends lamented, deciphering deadlines that feel like suggestions, navigating the bureaucratic maze, enduring delayed trains, and knowing when *yes* actually means *no* are all part of the Italian experience.

And yet Italy is also known for its world-class excellence. From automobiles to fashion, the Italian touch brings a unique blend of technical mastery and artistic flair. This excellence is not accidental—it results from a calculated focus on what Italians value most. On the one hand, Italy's public healthcare system is well regarded for providing quality medical care to all residents. On the other hand, Italy's postal service is notoriously slow and unreliable. While Italy's fashion industry is among the most influential globally, the country has been slower in developing a robust technological sector. Although the Italians have native cork oak trees and could have a thriving cork production industry like Portugal, they instead focus on producing world-class wine.

Lucilio Vanini, a sixteenth-century Italian philosopher, encapsulated this concept in his assertion that the greatest perfection lies in imperfection. The classic understanding of perfection assumes a fixed state in which nothing is left to improve. According to Vanini, a world without the potential for evolution would lack true perfection; it would be dead and static—a lifeless rather than flawless world. For him, perfection arises from imperfection due to its potential for development, just like a perfect painting doesn't strive to answer every question but instead gives room for the viewer's imagination to fill in the blanks. Artists are free to devote their attention to painting, their area of excellence, while leaving the task of interpretation to viewers. Despite official efforts to silence the ideas of Vanini, who considered himself a freethinker, the philosophy of embracing imperfection to achieve excellence has trickled down through the centuries, shaping the Italian way of life. The idea is not to achieve a life devoid of frustration but to recognize that to live an excellent life, we must let go of absolute perfection.

The Italian practice of intentional imperfection is reflected in this accord between sweet and sour—the appreciation that both are necessary for a rich, flavorful life. In fact, research on psychological resilience shows that those who embrace life's inherent imperfections with all its ups and downs exhibit greater mental well-being. By accepting life as an ever-changing cycle—good and bad, joyful and sad, fun and challenging—we become able to manage stress better and maintain robust mental health.

Intentional imperfection isn't about settling for less or not trying your best. Much like the Italians know they can't make some of the best wine and also make the best corks to close the bottles, intentional imperfection means being deliberate about where you invest your efforts, recognizing that you cannot be at the very top all the time and across all areas of life. It's about striving for sustainable excellence rather than fleeting perfection.

Ben Trosky was a highly successful bond manager—his fund ranked number one for the ten years he managed it. After retiring, Trosky shared the counterintuitive strategy that had driven his success. He explained that he consciously avoided striving for his fund to be the number one performer in any single year. Why? Because, in his experience, those who reached that top spot usually got there through reckless tactics. They took extreme risks, and even if they got lucky one year, their success was often short-lived.

Knowing full well that short-term results can be deceiving and that a brief snapshot of a performance track record holds little value, Trosky never tried to keep the top spot any one year but rather to place in the top 10 percent over ten years, aiming for long-term excellence rather than peak performance. That meant taking small, consistent swings, carefully balancing risk and reward. Trosky calls this way of investing *strategic mediocrity*. His thesis is that it is possible to be excellent over the long term by not investing in the highest-performing bonds over the short term. Rejecting the societal obsession with constant perfection, he argues that all-or-nothing, perfectionist approaches are often not the most successful.

Much like some investors who risk it all for short-term success, we often risk our mental health in the relentless pursuit of perfection. Yes, you might enjoy the thrill of being the top performer for a brief period, but at what cost? Striving to put 100 percent effort into everything you do is a recipe for burnout.

To be in the top decile over the long run requires being strategic about where to invest your energy. Instead of fast and furious, intentional imperfection is slow and steady. It sacrifices the thrill of short-term rewards for the serenity of sustainable success. As Trosky deliberately approached his investments, you, too, can be selective about how you invest your energy. At any given moment, ask yourself: *What is most important right now? In which domain do I strategically choose short-term mediocrity to enable long-term excellence?*

BETTER DONE THAN PERFECT

I once saw a parent post the following observation on Twitter: "It's wild to see the baby struggling with challenges like 'you have to take your hand out of your mouth if you want to use your hand for other things' and realize many adults still struggle with slightly more sophisticated versions of the same problems."

It may seem surprisingly simple, but the essence of intentional imperfection is accepting your limitations: you cannot expect to simultaneously excel at every target you set for yourself. To put this in the language of *Sesame Street*, it's the equivalent of the line, "You've got to put down the ducky if you want to play the saxophone."

For an entire year, my pact was to devote at least five hours per week to working on this book. It often ended up being many more hours, but I designed it this way because it was more flexible than a daily pact (e.g., "one hour per day") and allowed me to shift things around in my schedule if needed.

However, I made this pact while in the middle of my doctoral studies, prompting an honest conversation with my supervisors. Academia is a highly competitive environment where you're supposed to publish constantly, present your work at conferences, and teach several times a week. But I said, "I won't do a lot of teaching this year. I won't mentor undergraduates next summer. Not all my findings will be presented at conferences."

Solely focusing on my core studies and publishing the results meant I didn't perform many of the additional tasks expected from a top doctoral student. But I knew I had a limited amount of physical, cognitive, and emotional resources to contend with, and I chose intentional imperfection over joining the 50 percent of candidates who never complete their PhD.

Once there was a fantastic opportunity to submit a paper in a special issue. The topic exactly aligned with my research, but we found out about this opportunity only a couple of weeks before the deadline. I could have pushed through, working days and nights to finish writing the paper while honoring my book deadlines, but I didn't. Instead, I told my supervisors that I didn't have enough bandwidth. The paper was eventually published in another journal. Focusing on long-term excellence instead of trying to be perfect across the board allowed me to protect my mental health and to still deliver great work overall.

Many other people have found success in embracing intentional imperfection. Piotr Synowiec had a long-standing interest in learning to code. He wanted to build his own app. However, he knew that running his existing branding studio and learning to code would demand enormous effort, so he made a conscious choice about where to invest his energy.

Synowiec devoted most of his attention to his primary role at the branding studio. He was in the middle of a challenging project with a major cosmetics brand. His studio's responsibilities included rebranding over forty products and creating new bottles—a task that required dedication and near perfection.

But instead of altogether abandoning his coding aspirations, Synowiec chose the path of intentional imperfection. He didn't pressure himself to move as quickly as he might have liked. His pact was to code at least once a week. He started by simply taking online courses. Sometimes he would spend just ten minutes studying in the evening, and other times he would find only one hour in the entire week. As a result, it took him two years to learn how to code and another three years to build his first app.

Today, Synowiec is proud of himself for patiently completing this project and sees great value in the knowledge he gained. Through his journey, he managed to keep up his standards at the branding studio while slowly but surely building his app. He may not be celebrated in the tech media like other founders who "work like hell" to achieve all their objectives, but he did all this without sacrificing his mental health. Synowiec understood that it's not about always being the best at everything all the time. Excellence is a marathon, not a sprint.

By focusing on what truly matters in the moment and letting go of absolute perfection, you, too, can achieve sustainable success. To put the principles of intentional imperfection into practice, you just need to adjust those three ambition dials:

1. **Identify perfectionist patterns.** Before you can start embracing imperfection, you need to become aware of when and how you are unrealistically striving for perfection. If you feel stretched, write down your current commitments—all of them—and describe what success would look like for each.

2. **Challenge your unrealistic targets.** Looking at the list of highly ambitious objectives you have committed to is usually enough to convince you that you cannot possibly accomplish them all at once. But you can dig a bit deeper if you need more proof. How much effort would it require to complete each of these projects to your standards? Do you really have enough hours in the day to do everything on this list? Or have you already subconsciously decided to forgo other activities like socializing or working out? Pretend you are helping a friend out and be brutally honest with yourself.

3. **Choose progress over perfection.** This is where the intentional part comes into play. Decide on the parts of your life and work where you will drop the ball to achieve excellence in other areas. It doesn't have to

be forever; maybe you'll decide to focus on a certain aspect of your life for the next week, or perhaps it will be only for today or tonight.

Accepting that not everything has to be perfect leads to a less pressured yet more fulfilling life. Unattainable standards are replaced with a heightened focus on what matters. Frustration turns into calm exploration. Setbacks become creative constraints.

Consider the ancient Japanese art of kintsugi. When pottery breaks, the typical response is to repair it in a manner that masks the damage or discard it altogether. Kintsugi, on the other hand, embraces these imperfections by lacquering over the cracks with gold or silver. This doesn't just mend the broken pottery; it visually accentuates the breakage. The result is a narrative artifact that celebrates the beauty emerging from imperfection.

In 2016, an entire exhibition at the Getty Museum, titled *Drawing: The Art of Change*, featured artwork that showcased the ways artists let new ideas arise from imperfection. Without erasers, which were not invented before the eighteenth century, artists had to work with emerging shapes and unexpected results to move forward. "An error in an artwork creates a feeling that something is possible; it is an open window to something we do not control," as Cedric van Eenoo beautifully puts it. "This space where the unknown becomes reachable is precious: we are to be surprised and astonished by the poetry of the unexpected."

Indeed, intentional imperfection often becomes fuel for creativity. Once we accept that we will never be able to do everything perfectly, we may start thinking about innovative ways to work within our limitations. As your mindset changes, you may see progress and opportunities emerge from failures or "falling short," discovering that a less-than-perfect approach is actually a more creative one, and that constraints can unlock exciting new possibilities.

Rather than risk your sanity in a mad dash for perfection, you can enjoy meandering along the road to excellence—no matter how imperfect the path looks in the here and now.

REACT

Collaborate with Uncertainty

7

✐ *Creating Growth Loops*

In September 2022, I was in London, sitting on the sofa in front of my TV, riveted as Eliud Kipchoge broke—again—the marathon world record in Berlin. What many people do not know about one of the fastest marathoners in history is his habit of keeping a detailed diary. This diary is not just a log of his physical training; it also includes notes on his mental state, observations about his environment, and reflections on his performance. In an interview with *Outside,* he explains: "I document the time, the kilometers, the massage, the exercises, the shoes I'm using, the feeling about those shoes. Everything." All of these constitute crucial parameters for him to consider and to tweak.

Kipchoge intuitively understands that making progress requires two essential components: trial and error. The trial part of the loop involves taking action with limited information; it requires a willingness to step into the unknown and explore possibilities. The error part involves observing the results and making adjustments based on that data. If you don't do both, you don't grow.

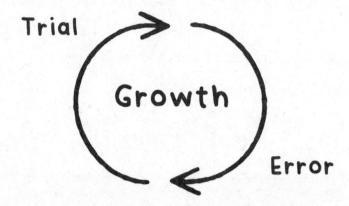

As Nassim Taleb has put it, in complex systems—"ones in which we have little visibility of the chains of cause-consequences"—trial and error beats a linear approach designed for a specific target. This iterative model is inspired by nature itself. Nature adapts in response to environmental feedback and evolves through cycles of experimentation.

Polina Marinova Pompliano, founder of *The Profile* and author of *Hidden Genius,* also understands the two immutable sides of experimentation: "You could burn out if you consistently do the exact same thing," she told me. "Every year, I sit down and I review the feedback, both qualitative and quantitative. I reflect and I notice: *that's interesting, this is what people like, this is what they said last year, this is how I feel about it* . . . It's important to bake in moments of reflection."

Trial and error are inseparable. Without the willingness to try, we wouldn't have the opportunity to learn from our mistakes and refine our trajectory. And without reflection, we would repeat the same error in an infinite number of trials. That would keep us busy, but it wouldn't really help us grow. For sustainable success, we need to pause to learn from each repetition; to make small adjustments each time, picking up new abilities and knowledge along the way.

When we use trial and error, we set in motion a series of growth loops where progress emerges in conversation with our environment. Each cycle adds a layer of learning to how we understand ourselves and the world around us. Instead of an external destination, our aspirations become fuel for transformation. We don't *go* in circles; we *grow* in circles.

Our ancestors instinctively knew of this circular model of growth. In many cultures, the wheel is a symbol of growth and success. It combines the idea of progress and wholeness: It is complete, and yet it keeps on moving. It represents the perpetual change and transitory nature of life. The cyclic ages of Hindu cosmology, the wheel of life in Buddhism . . . The dynamic dance of the Chinese yin and yang also recognizes cycles of life that encompass opposites, the dual craving we have for discovery and comfort, and the desire to find balance in accommodating both phases into our lives. In Greek mythology, the phoenix cyclically regenerates so that every ending is a new beginning.

This cyclic, experimental model also aligns with the way our mind naturally works. The brain is thought to be built on a giant perception-action cycle, with a circular flow of information between the self and the environment, where the system constantly conveys whether a signal should be intensified or stopped. In essence, we don't just set our mind on a target and blindly power through. Instead, our brain converts the information it perceives into action; it uses feedback loops to constantly adjust our trajectory as we make progress. This feedback loop is so well established, it is considered the theoretical cornerstone of most modern theories of learning.

When you start looking, you will notice many of our greatest achievements can be traced back to such iterative cycles of trial and error. The scientific method relies on formulating hypotheses, testing them, and incorporating the results into the design of future experiments. Sports teams commit to a strategy, apply it during a game, and keep on adapting their approach through each cycle of training and competition.

For instance, the soccer team at FC Barcelona experimented with many different formations and playing styles over the course of several seasons to develop their signature "tiki-taka" style of play, which involves rapid short passes and fluid movement. Chefs experiment by adding an ingredient, tasting it to see if it works, and keeping or discarding the change depending on the result over many attempts. As famous chef Julia Child said: "If everything doesn't happen quite the way you'd like, it doesn't make too much difference because you can fix it." In all these examples, "failure" is inherent in the process: it is not feared but embraced as a tool that directs us toward the next step in our journey of discovery.

THE MIND'S SWISS ARMY KNIFE

When you consciously turn your thoughts inward, you can evaluate the impact of your past actions and consider potential paths forward with more clarity. A time-honored technique embodies the kind of continuous self-reflection I'm talking about: the ancient and powerful practice of metacognition. This is the distinctly human ability to reflect on your own learning process to synthesize insights, appreciate how far you've come, and determine where to focus next—but not enough of us are using it.

While introspection is simply noticing your thoughts and emotions, metacognition involves both awareness and analysis. It's like having a wise inner coach who observes the game and shares strategies that are most likely to lead to smoother victory next time. It is not merely the realization that you're struggling or thriving but the ability to step back and understand why, asking: *What should I try next?*

Metacognition ensures your choices aren't made on impulse or in a bubble, but in conversation with both your inner self and the wider world. It allows you to parse what you have accomplished with clear eyes; to assess what worked, what didn't, how you really feel; and to appreciate the view from where you now stand.

Our ancestors' daily routines included organic opportunities to shape their inner world—on long walks, in meditative moments while completing repetitive tasks such as sewing and tending to crops, or in nightly reflection when praying before bed. But we in the present day have largely lost those quiet natural pauses. Instead, we grind on a near-constant flood of social media and emails. This leaves little space for thinking, let alone *thinking about thinking.*

This shutdown carries serious repercussions: research shows that, without metacognition, we are often unaware of the factors influencing our own choices and behaviors. In the absence of this internal discourse, we don't pay enough attention to extrapolate our experience into the future, and the wheel of trial and error doesn't lead to improvement.

In essence, metacognition is curiosity directed at your inner world—your thoughts, your emotions, your beliefs. It empowers you to be the master of your mind, providing you with the tools to shape these inner experiences in a way that brings you closer to your aspirations.

The more data you have to reflect on, the greater the insights gained to excel amid uncertainty. For example, when you notice an instinctive response and pause to consider it, you're then able to separate it from the tangle of other factors that may be in play. At that point you can evaluate whether it is a response you want to act upon.

Consider Barbara Oakley, who had a deep aversion to math and science as a child, believing she wasn't "wired" for them. It wasn't until she was in her mid-twenties and joined the army that Oakley saw firsthand the importance of understanding systems, which sparked her interest in engineering. She started from scratch, taking remedial algebra at a community college. As she delved into her studies, Oakley developed various metacognitive strategies to aid her learning. She realized the need to balance times of intense concentration (focused mode) with those of mental relaxation (diffuse mode) to solve problems efficiently. Those metacognitive strategies were crucial for Oakley's learning journey. She is now a professor of engineering, and the techniques she developed led her to co-create the wildly popular online course "Learning How to Learn," which has been taken by millions of students worldwide. Her story highlights how gaining insight into your own learning and thinking can lead to remarkable transformation.

Metacognition is for good reason often referred to as the forgotten secret to success. It is the skill that allows a student to recognize they're unprepared for an exam and take corrective action, or an athlete like Eliud Kipchoge to understand the importance of not just how fast he's running but also how his shoes feel during a run. Metacognition is also helpful for gaining clarity in everyday work situations. As marketer Leo Sadeq told me, "We deal with ten thousand things at a time in the office. Metacognition gives me clarity of thought and creative space to think. It's a way to assess whether I'm heading in the right direction."

The secret to designing growth loops is not better knowledge or skills, but your ability to think about your own thinking, question your automatic responses, and know your mind. That's the metacognitive edge: it equips you with the skills to be both the actor and the director in the unfolding story of your life. By reflecting on the past, you can better decode the future.

A SIMPLE METACOGNITIVE TOOL

Metacognition can be applied in countless ways to help us discover what's next, whether it's in our careers, health, or relationships. This is partly why it's one of the most popular modules I teach at Ness Labs. But the most cited reason this module changes students' lives is a simple tool I created to incorporate metacognition into your everyday life. The tool is called Plus Minus Next, and it does what it says on the tin with just three columns; positive observations go in the first column (Plus), negative observations in the second column (Minus), and plans for what's next in the last column (Next).*

Plus Minus Next is a versatile starter kit for metacognition. Esteban Balderas, a content creator in Mexico who has

---

* You can download a printable Plus Minus Next template here: https://nesslabs.com/pmn.

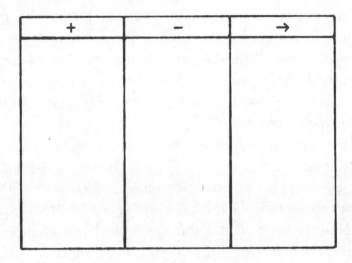

+	−	→

had a weekly Plus Minus Next practice for more than two years, considers it the cornerstone of his personal growth. "Even if I have the worst week, I can save five minutes to respond to some questions and benefit from the short reflection," he told me. Just a few of the course corrections he's made in the past year thanks to Plus Minus Next include making changes at home to support better habits, scheduling more time to be with friends, and letting go of some good projects that were getting in the way of great projects. "Being able to make small adjustments every week is something that you can't stop doing once you see the compound effect," he said.

Plus Minus Next is what binds action with reflection. It's the feedback after practice, the thinking that comes after doing, the debugging of life as it unfolds.

You can use whichever medium you prefer, but I recommend trying it out on paper the first time. Write the date at the top of a page and draw three columns. At the top of each column, write a plus sign for what worked, a minus sign for what didn't go so well, and an arrow for what you plan to do next.

Then fill it with experiences from the past week. Any experience constitutes valid information to include in your Plus Minus Next review. The idea is to capture a snapshot of your mind. That includes celebrations, questions, emotions—all viewed from a metacognitive perspective.

- **Plus.** Write down any accomplishment that made you proud. These could be largely work-based, but don't neglect other areas of your life such as relationships, hobbies, and homelife. Your achievements can be big or small, such as completing a project at work or learning a new skill, or small daily victories such as maintaining a consistent exercise routine. Reflect on moments that brought joy, such as special occasions, positive feedback you've received, time spent with loved ones, or even time spent alone. You could also more generally capture what you are grateful for in your life, ranging from meaningful relationships to your health or the comforts of your home.

- **Minus.** Identify any challenges or obstacles you faced, whether it was a difficult task at work, an unexpected setback, or an opportunity you missed. Maybe you experienced a misunderstanding in a personal or professional interaction. Maybe there are tasks you intended to complete but didn't. Acknowledge any mistakes you made, biases you noticed, decisions you regretted. This is also where you can note any areas of your life you feel were neglected, such as personal relationships, hobbies, or self-care. Keep track of when you strayed from your healthy habits, such as skipping workouts, eating unhealthily, or not getting enough sleep. If you experienced persistent negative emotions such as stress, anxiety, or frustration, jot these down as well.

- **Next.** Use the insights from both the Plus and Minus columns to shape your actions for the upcoming period. Consider strategies to foster more of the positive observations listed in the Plus column. This might involve protecting your time for work that brings you joy, seeking resources to acquire new skills, or finding ways to deepen the relationships that matter to you. Simultaneously, think about constructive ways to address the negative observations from the Minus column. You could plan to tackle an unfinished task, set time aside for an area of your life that needs more attention, attempt to break a bad habit, or commit to one activity that supports your well-being.

You don't need to rank achievements, challenges, and next steps in order of importance. You also don't necessarily need to tie next week's plans to what didn't work the previous week. Not everything needs to be fixed; not every problem needs a solution. This is especially the case for one-off challenges. Acknowledging them is enough to move on.

Thoughts about your pact might show up here, but the tool is holistic, not just to evaluate how your experiments are going. Let your mind flow without forcing an artificial structure besides those three simple columns. Here is a real example compiled from the Ness Labs community.

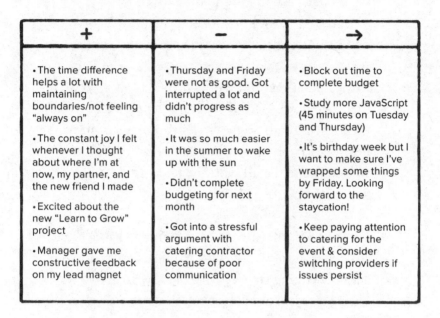

+	-	→
• The time difference helps a lot with maintaining boundaries/not feeling "always on" • The constant joy I felt whenever I thought about where I'm at now, my partner, and the new friend I made • Excited about the new "Learn to Grow" project • Manager gave me constructive feedback on my lead magnet	• Thursday and Friday were not as good. Got interrupted a lot and didn't progress as much • It was so much easier in the summer to wake up with the sun • Didn't complete budgeting for next month • Got into a stressful argument with catering contractor because of poor communication	• Block out time to complete budget • Study more JavaScript (45 minutes on Tuesday and Thursday) • It's birthday week but I want to make sure I've wrapped some things by Friday. Looking forward to the staycation! • Keep paying attention to catering for the event & consider switching providers if issues persist

Plus Minus Next is simple, but it is based on centuries of practical wisdom. The ancient Greeks talked of *praxis,* or "thinking in action." Present-day researchers call it reflection in action. You may call it thinking on your feet. Plus Minus Next works because it's fast, flexible, and future-focused:

- **Fast.** Filling your weekly page shouldn't take more than five minutes. A few bullet points, and you're done. The column that should take the longest is the one titled "Next," as you should take some time to reflect on what happened the past week to decide where to focus during the following week.

- **Flexible.** Life is complex, but a lot of reflection methods are overly rigid. Every area of our lives is interconnected, so the way we reflect on it should be as well. "Abandon the urge to simplify everything, to look for formulas and easy answers, and begin to think multidimensionally," said American psychiatrist M. Scott Peck. The Plus Minus Next method works for all areas of your life; there's no need to separate the personal from the professional. Some weeks you may not have much to say about work, and that's fine. Other weeks, it may be all work-related items. That's fine, too.

- **Future-focused.** Instead of dwelling too much on stuff that didn't work, Plus Minus Next is about acknowledging the negative in a constructive way. Didn't finish that project you were planning on shipping last week? Don't beat yourself up; just make it a priority next week.

Many people use Plus Minus Next for their weekly review. "I found it a great way to express gratitude and to realize that last week was really productive, as opposed to the Sunday gloom of looking forward to the next week," physician and researcher Dr. Scott Wagers told me. Like Wagers, I also enjoy doing my Plus Minus Next review on Sunday evening when it's quiet at home, but some people do it on Monday morning to start the week on the right foot.

As Balderas puts it, "On New Year's Eve, we usually think about our lives: what went well, what didn't, and what we want to accomplish next year. But if you only think about that once a year, your life is not going to improve much. What if you could feel that burst of inspiration every week? That is the usefulness of Plus Minus Next. Without much effort, you can have a moment of reflection that will inspire you to take actions that will improve your life. Take a look at what you did last week, reflect on it, and take a better step this week."

Plus Minus Next also works great alongside daily journaling, whether you use bullet journaling, morning pages, or simply free writing. Some people start with journaling, then collate key observations in the Plus Minus Next columns, or go the other way around and expand on the observations with journaling. Plus Minus Next can also stand on its own for those who struggle to journal on a consistent basis.

Some of my students use it in a more targeted way, to evaluate specific events or ongoing processes. Yina Huang, a consultant based in New York, used the tool to evaluate the planning and execution of a baby shower, so that she'd have the insights to apply to her next event. Later, focused on the care and development of her months-old infant, Huang used Plus Minus Next to monitor her daughter's quickly changing needs and to improve along the way. The tool helped her notice, for example, that bedtime was a struggle on the days when her daughter didn't have enough time during the day to expend energy.

I also use Plus Minus Next with my team as a way for us to reflect at the end of each week. Each team member brings their filled-out Plus Minus Next to our 1:1 meetings, allowing us to have structured discussions about their achievements, challenges, and plans. It ensures that we regularly reflect on what we can do differently moving forward and helps keep everyone aligned and motivated.

Finally, Plus Minus Next is a great tool for conducting an

annual review. Each year, at the end of December, I sit down, go through all my weekly reviews, and write a retrospective, which I publish in my newsletter. I get to see all that I have accomplished, all that didn't come to fruition, and all the questions that remain to explore for the following year.

Whether you use it to parent an infant, train for a marathon, or run a small business (or perhaps all three), you're in charge. Choosing the right frequency for Plus Minus Next can be an experiment in and of itself.

Plus Minus Next is a powerful way to inject metacognition into your daily life and work. It isn't about making big changes, crafting five-year plans, or finding your purpose. Instead, it focuses on incremental adjustments that compound over time. You can identify what you want more of and proactively focus your attention on these sources of growth. Equally, a difficult interaction can become an opportunity to define your preferred communication style. A failed project launch can offer insights into team dynamics. A double-booked appointment can make you wonder about your current workload.

What went well? What didn't go so well? What should I try next? By periodically asking yourself those questions, you get to learn about yourself and evolve with intention instead of letting change happen on autopilot.

MAKING GOOD MISTAKES

Leonardo da Vinci is well known for his many masterpieces, including the most famous painting in the world, which sits in the Louvre in my city of birth. As a child, I remember looking at the flawless painting of the *Mona Lisa* (which is much smaller than you would expect) and trying to see if her eyes would indeed follow me as I moved through the room. Leonardo is also known for the plethora of inventions sketched in his notebooks, such as predecessors to the parachute and the helicopter, and even a self-propelled cart, which is considered the ancestor of the modern automobile.

What people may not know is how messy and iterative Leonardo's creative process was. Scholars have described how he would start sketching ideas without a full understanding of how they worked, using the mistakes he discovered to propel his thinking forward. His drawings were in fact so often covered in smears and stains that his inky fingerprints have been used to identify some of his work centuries after his death. Still, he kept them all.

Metacognition might feel uncomfortable at times. It's easy to write about what went well, regardless of the specifics that led to that success. It is more difficult to write about what went wrong. And it is even harder when, as is sometimes the case, we ourselves must take sole responsibility for why things didn't go so well.

To err is human. We fall prey to miscalculations and mishaps. These errors can range from minor oversights that are barely noticeable to more significant blunders. Not all errors are obvious; some are diffuse assumptions, subtly influencing our actions. Even when we do recognize a mistake, we might brush it off or try to avoid it in the future without addressing its underlying causes.

Any attempt to avoid mistakes altogether would be fruitless, but we can choose how we respond when they occur. Daniel Dennett—one of my favorite philosophers—wrote that we should strive to make good mistakes. Good mistakes prompt us to reflect and refine our approach, which increases our momentum. They are the ones we learn from and that make us grow.

For the longest time, I was a night owl. My most productive and creative hours were after sunset. But when I quit drinking alcohol, my body suddenly shifted gears. I now feel sleepy right after dinner and wake up before sunrise without an alarm. When I noticed the change, I asked myself: *Do I like this or not?*

When we start digging into the ways we evolve, the answer often is something like: *It's complicated.* In my case, the change should have been good, but I was exhausted. It turned out that my body clock had shifted, but I hadn't adapted my work patterns. I would wake up before sunrise, journal, then start working and keep on going until dinner, routinely putting in twelve-hour shifts without noticing.

Well, my body was certainly noticing. And metacognition helped me pay attention. Instead of persisting with that mistake, I made some changes. I now take a longer break in the middle of the day (with a short nap if I'm working from home that day) and finish work much earlier to go for a walk, read, take care of chores around the house, or, sometimes, simply do nothing.

Because we seldom bring those errors to conscious awareness, we miss the opportunity to grow from them. Change is unintentional; adaptation is accidental. But there is so much to learn from our mistakes; we should learn to fall in love with them. Fundamentally, Plus Minus Next is a tool for making good mistakes. While the pact allows us to commit to action, Plus Minus Next allows us to evaluate our actions. It helps us celebrate our accomplishments and learn from our mistakes. Only through combined action and reflection can we achieve meaningful growth: trial and error create a feedback loop of guaranteed learning—a successful cycle of experimentation.

By combining your pact with a metacognitive practice, you have now created your own life laboratory, equipped with everything you need to learn through deliberate action and reflection—an approach based on experimenting, assessing what worked, what didn't, and what to change next.

8

⇇ *The Secret to Better Decisions*

Picture this: You did it. After days, weeks, or perhaps months of consistent effort, the trial period is over. Your pact is complete. You published the hundredth blog post, wrote daily in your journal, or attended improv classes eight weeks in a row. Or maybe you didn't carry out the experiment as planned. Either way, it doesn't matter. What matters is that you collected data and dedicated time for reflection throughout the experiment.

Now you get to decide what your next growth loop will look like. If everything has been going well, you may be dreaming about all the ways you will build on your accomplishment. If your pact was to write a five-hundred-word journal entry every day, you're already envisioning a book project. If your pact was to spend forty-five minutes on Sundays learning how to edit videos, you're thinking about how to become a YouTube star.

When we reach the end of a loop, culturally inflected ambition spurs us to raise the stakes, even if that's not what we really want. It's an understandable impulse, particularly in the professional realm. Our economy is built not on the notion of *enough* but on the notion of *more*. Bigger, better, higher, faster. We want to capitalize on momentum or prove that the hard work was "worth it." We press on to the next level.

But completing a pact doesn't mean you must now strive for more. Instead, you're at a crossroads, where different paths are available. All things considered, there are three viable alternative routes for this transition:

- **Persist.** The wind is in your sails. You are enjoying your ongoing experiment and starting to reap its rewards, learning more about yourself and the world around you. All you need to do now is ride the wave of your current momentum and prolong your pact.

- **Pause.** Whether it is draining too much energy, negatively affecting your personal or professional life, or clashing with other commitments, the experiment isn't going well. As a result, you want to quit your pact or at least put it on hold.

- **Pivot.** The experiment could benefit from some tweaks, whether that is increasing or decreasing its scope or changing your tools and tactics. Though the fundamentals of the pact will remain the same, you sense a slight course correction could be beneficial.

We would like to think ourselves able to consider these three options rationally, but neuroscientists have found that our choices are significantly influenced by the manner in which options are presented, and that decision-making can be irrationally driven by emotional responses. So let's have a closer look at each option, and then use a simple tool so you can ensure your decisions are a true reflection of the data currently at your disposal.

PERSIST: TAKING A STAND

In January 2024, I heard myself say "I'm terrible at meditation. It just doesn't work for me." By now, you can probably guess what my reaction was when those words came out of my mouth. "Is that true? Am I really bad at meditation?" And I started a new pact: meditating for fifteen minutes a day for fifteen days. The experiment was a resounding success. Not only did I not miss a day, but I actually enjoyed it.

As soon as I completed the last day, my mind started racing. I wanted to try longer meditations, maybe one or two hours a day. I started looking up formal meditation training. I researched some intensive online courses, which required spending an entire weekend without outside contact. I also found a ten-day silent retreat not far from where I lived. Fortunately, I snapped out of it and remembered that I loved my pact as it was.

Why do so many people blaze past the obvious option to simply stay the course? I've consciously chosen the term *persist* to describe this option because it implies a decisive and daring move—which in our world of hustle, it is. Every time I decide to simply persist with my current direction, it feels like taking a stand. We've been conditioned to think of enjoying forward momentum as coasting or taking our foot off the gas, and what should be seen as a healthy pushback against the cult of more is frowned upon.

However, to equate stasis with failure is a modern invention and a cultural myth. In many indigenous societies around the world, success is based on sustainability and harmony with the environment, measured by the ability to maintain a balanced relationship with nature and to ensure the well-being of the community for generations to come. In medieval guilds, where mastering a skill and producing high-quality goods were highly valued, the focus was on maintaining a standard of excellence rather than constant growth. And of course, from Taoism to Buddhism, many Asian philosophies emphasize the importance of balance rather than the endless pursuit of more. Persisting with the same pact creates ample room for rest and reflection—and thus for self-discovery—allowing us to sustain and appreciate what we have instead of always chasing more.

And yet because it may require you to defy cultural expectations, merely persisting can turn into a bold assertion of what you value. Take the case of Bill Watterson, the creator of the beloved comic strip *Calvin and Hobbes*, who had made a pact to produce daily strips that resonated deeply with readers. He enjoyed the work and had no plans of stopping. However, as the popularity of his work grew, he faced mounting pressure to capitalize on its success by expanding into other forms of media, including turning his characters into merchandise. While his editor saw expansion as the logical next step in the pursuit of maximum growth, Watterson chose to stick to his original commitment. After intense negotiations, he secured a contract that ensured his creative autonomy and protected *Calvin and Hobbes* from being turned into mere commodities. Watterson effectively prioritized safeguarding the integrity of his creative work over expanding the project's scope in pursuit of more money.

Or take Maria Popova, who has been writing weekly essays about literature, art, and philosophy for her blog *The Marginalian* for about two decades. During this time, the digital landscape evolved with new platforms and the potential to grow her brand by churning out more frequent but shallower content. But Popova stayed committed to her pact of publishing long-form content every week, demonstrating that she values her original source of curiosity—a deep search for meaning—and is unwilling to dilute it to expand her reach.

When you're not playing a game of leveling up and chasing linear goals, persistence—showing up consistently over a long period of time, long enough that you can start seeing the compound interest in your work—can be a powerful differentiator.

PAUSE: TAKING A BREAK

According to Buddhist legend, on the night Gautama Buddha was conceived, his mother dreamed of a white elephant. And so for many centuries, white elephants were sacred in many Southeast Asian countries. Receiving a white elephant as a gift from a monarch was a great honor. But it was also a curse, as the animal was extremely expensive to maintain, protected from labor by local laws, and impossible to give away. People were stuck with this beautiful but useless possession with ruinous maintenance costs.

Most of us have at least once created a white elephant for

ourselves, whether it's staying in a job despite feeling miserable, continuing to invest in a failing business because we've already spent lots of money trying to make it work, or not breaking up because we've been in a relationship with someone for so long already. In an absurd escalation of commitment, we keep putting in the effort even if the outcomes become increasingly negative, as long as our behavior aligns with our previous decisions and actions.

The stigma attached to quitting often clouds our judgment and can keep us tethered to a project that drains our physical, cognitive, and emotional resources. A powerful barrier to taking a break or abandoning a project is the sunk cost fallacy: the irrational reasoning that further investment—be it time, money, or effort—must be made simply because of the initial investment, regardless of the current and future value of that project. We have poured so much energy and hope into a project that it feels impossible to withdraw. We are also scared of what people would think.

That's why the bravest thing you can do, sometimes, is to admit that a course of action is no longer serving you and to bow out gracefully. As serial entrepreneur Seth Godin puts it: "Quitting the projects that don't go anywhere is essential if you want to stick out the right ones." Every moment you invest in a direction that no longer resonates is a moment you could have invested elsewhere, in a commitment that could offer you more fulfillment. Maybe there's another skill you could learn or a project you could start, or even some much-needed leisure time you could enjoy.

I call the quitting option *pause*, again with intention. This not only eases the stigma of throwing in the towel but also reflects what quitting often is: a strategic temporary decision. Curious minds understand that the future holds infinite and unimaginable possibilities, including the potential to restart an abandoned experiment.

I once started a YouTube channel and made a pact to publish one video every week until the end of that year. This pact proved particularly challenging: I was nervous about speaking on camera, overthinking every little video edit, and found it hard to translate my written words into a visual format. The stress was exacerbated when I started my PhD studies and had less time to dedicate to researching and scripting videos. After about six months, I weighed the pros and cons of persisting, pausing, or pivoting. Because of the combination of external and internal factors, it was evident that I needed to pause this pact.

What I hadn't predicted at the time was that my curiosity about YouTube would be piqued again two years later. This time, instead of trying to control every step of the creative process, I hired a videographer to help me edit the recordings. The pact itself hadn't changed—it was still to publish a weekly video—but my approach had changed. Trusting that a professional would know how to turn my raw materials into an engaging video alleviated much of the pressure, and recording became a joy. This time, I successfully completed my pact.

Other times, the end is the end. In April 1994, Watterson began a sabbatical that would last until the end of the year. Upon his return, he announced that *Calvin and Hobbes* would conclude at the end of 1995. Sharing his belief that he had achieved everything he wanted within the medium, Watterson said he intended to work on future projects at a slower pace with fewer creative concessions. The final strip ran on December 31, 1995, and showed Calvin and Hobbes sledding down a snowy hill, with Calvin exclaiming, "Let's go exploring!"

When your aim is to learn, quitting is not an admission of failure. It's an exercise in adaptability. There is no point in rigidly clinging to an obsolete path when everything else has changed. Pausing is the appropriate move when the data you've collected strongly indicates a new course of action, when your efforts are negatively affecting your physical or mental health, or when there is no joy or clear value in continuing.

PIVOT: TAKING A TURN

On the evening of September 8, 1923, Captain Edward H. Watson and Lieutenant Commander Donald T. Hunter were leading a fleet of warships on an engineering run off the coast of Southern California. The exercise was to simulate wartime conditions, which meant that maintaining the fastest possible speed was predefined as a hard requirement for success.

The fog was thick that day. Because of the poor visibility, Hunter had been navigating by dead reckoning, an age-old technique that involves estimating your current position by using a previously determined position and incorporating estimates of speed and direction. It was not the most precise way to proceed, but Hunter was a veteran mariner and felt he had a good idea of their location.

Just as Watson and Hunter were ready to give the order to turn left into the Santa Barbara Channel, they received a signal from a navy radio station on the coast, indicating a position for the USS *Delphy* that was completely different from the one they had determined with compass and speed estimates. "Impossible bearing!" Hunter shouted, as immortalized by the radio recording of that momentous day.

Faced with conflicting data, the captain and the lieutenant commander could have chosen to slow down and take measurements of water depths, prioritizing safety over speed and real-time data over instinct. But slowing down would have required them to abandon the predefined parameters for success, so they didn't. The USS *Delphy* ran aground, leading six other ships to destruction in a disastrous procession. Twenty-three sailors died that day. Known as the Honda Point disaster, it was the largest ever peacetime loss of American navy ships.

While in a liminal space—a thick fog that obscured both their exact location and their direction—Watson and Hunter decided to ignore new information and stick to their plan. In a talk for the Long Now Foundation, Paul Saffo, professor at Stanford University, noted that "the real lesson here is, about uncertainty, when the *Delphy* skipper hit the rocks along with those . . . other destroyers, it happened because he narrowed his cone of uncertainty at the very moment that the data was screaming to widen it."

Staying the course can be the better option in many situations. However, persisting, pausing, and pivoting are equally valid choices when made deliberately. The key is to remain open to cues that suggest a need for a change in your thinking.

Refocusing on the hypothesis underlying your current experiment can be helpful. Do you feel like you have enough data to answer your research question? If you're still curious to know the answer and some changes are required to complete your pact, then it is worth considering a pivot. Remember that the primary goal is to learn, grow, and discover more about yourself and the world.

When you decide that a course correction is needed, your next step is to understand how much change is necessary.

You could make a small tweak or a big revamp. For instance, a musician who has committed to practicing for two hours daily could make a minor adjustment to their practice schedule by switching from mornings to evenings due to new work commitments. Or a major overhaul might involve reducing the commitment to one hour a day because of a change in their family dynamics.

The key is to ask yourself: *What part of the pact can be adjusted so I can keep learning and growing despite changing circumstances?*

The 100 articles pact at the inception of Ness Labs was based on writing one article every weekday—or five articles a week. This was a good fit at the time; my only other commitments were my neuroscience studies, which I was completing part time, and one consulting contract that required only a few hours of work every week. Writing brought me lots of joy, so once I completed the first pact, I decided to persist for a while.

But as the newsletter started taking off, other opportunities arose—building a community, coaching, hosting workshops. After a while, it became evident that I needed to scale my pact down. I first reduced my commitment to three articles a week, then two. And when I started writing this book, I scaled it down again to only one article a week. The result? Not only is the newsletter still going after five years—which in and of itself is something I'm proud of—but it has engagement rates ten times above average.

Crucially, I'm still having tons of fun.

By staying nimble and making adjustments when required, you can keep your experiment on track through changing tides. Be iterative, not dogmatic: approach this process with the humility of a scientist, not the rigidity of an officer following orders. Few aspects of life are like a military exercise in which speed defines success. As long as you're learning and growing, it doesn't matter if your route meanders. Your pact should evolve along with you.

BROADENING THE DECISION FRAME

Unlike Watson, you need to pay attention to the right signals to steer in the most advantageous direction. But which direction, especially when you don't have a finish line in mind?

Very few of us are equipped with a balanced, holistic approach to integrate many signals in our decision-making, particularly under pressure. We use what researchers call a narrow decision frame, based on the most salient objective, the first option that lands on the table, and the expected state of the world. We often rely too much on either external or internal signals, resulting in an incomplete view. People who focus on external signals try to be rational, while those who focus on internal ones tend to follow their intuition. Both approaches ignore vital information.

Most formal decision-making methods fail to correct for these biases. Take, for example, the sturdy rite of listing pros and cons. Even Benjamin Franklin advocated for this approach. In a 1772 letter to Joseph Priestley, he wrote: "My way is to divide half a sheet of paper by a line into two columns, writing over the one *Pro*, and over the other *Con*. Then during three or four days consideration, I put down under the different heads short hints of the different motives that at different times occur to me for or against the measure."

The pros-and-cons list masquerades as a dependable,

objective tool, seemingly protecting us from shallow decisions. After recording all the positives and negatives of a choice, the thinking goes, you then can weigh them carefully against each other, with reason triumphing over impulse. But is that really the case?

Internal factors, such as our emotions, readily operate as an unconscious filter influencing the content of each column. For example, if you want to quit a pact but feel guilty about it, you may emphasize more cons than actually exist to retroactively validate your desire to stop. Additionally, the focus on measured, rational thinking may lead you to overemphasize external signals, ignoring valid emotional factors.

In other words, a pros-and-cons list often teases out all the reasons you think something should be wrong or right, without ever digging into whether something is wrong or right *for you* and *why*. Simply listing the pros and cons doesn't capture the full range of motivations that drive your choices. Rather than illuminating what you really want, social psychologist Timothy D. Wilson warns, such lists can provide plausible-sounding but hollow reasons to pursue choices that do not reflect your authentic needs and desires.

To better assess your situation, practice decision framing: Widen your cone of uncertainty and explicitly take into account not only external signals but also internal ones. Once again, consider your life as would an anthropologist—with systematic curiosity.

External signals typically have a visible impact. An exciting new job, changes to a work timeline, kids starting school, taking care of a loved one . . . These and other changing conditions in the outside world may lead you to rethink your path. Internal signals may not be as obvious. Perhaps a commitment that once excited you now feels like a chore, or what felt ambitious in a good way now feels overwhelming. Such internal signals are as important as external ones, and they, too, require critical evaluation. Acting on gut feelings can be treacherous, especially when complacency, as in Hunter's case, can lead us to dismiss "impossible" data.

Both external and internal signals influence our actions, so it's essential to put equal effort into articulating them. You can capture all these signals and broaden your decision frame using a simple Steering Sheet:

External Signals

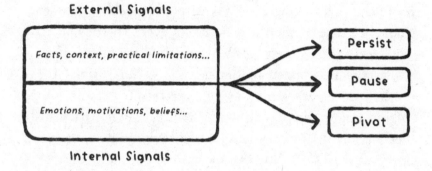

Facts, context, practical limitations...

Emotions, motivations, beliefs...

Persist

Pause

Pivot

Internal Signals

Ask yourself the following questions:

- **External signals:** These include facts, contextual information, and practical limitations. How does your pact fit with your current circumstances? Is it manageable or is it in conflict with your other commitments? Are there other things in your life that are using, or need, more emotional energy? Has anything in the world changed?

- **Internal signals:** These include your emotions, motivations, and other mental states. How do you feel about your pact now? Is it still fulfilling, or has it become a source of tension? What is your level of self-confidence? What other beliefs and feelings can you identify when you think about your pact?

Once you have listed all the external and internal signals that might influence your decision, you can take a step back and consider this much fuller picture, allowing you to evaluate the choices with a clearer mind and ultimately make a more informed choice as to whether you want to persist, pause, or pivot.

No matter how good your tool or deliberative your thought process, one thing never changes: There is no right choice. If you're used to zero-sum thinking, that point of view may frustrate you. But it's almost impossible to fail when you see everything as an experiment. In a life of experimentation, there is no wrong choice, either. A pact isn't a destination. It's a path you walk to discover more about yourself and the world. Success and failure are fluid constructs, not fixed labels. If you simply keep going as is, it means you found an ideal groove—amazing! If you decide to stop, it means this direction didn't feel good—now you know!

The only failure is to confuse mindless movement with mindful momentum. As long as you keep on adapting, learning, and growing, you are winning.

9

✦ *How to Dance with Disruption*

Once upon a time, in a small village in ancient China, a farmer's horse ran away into the wild. The neighbors, wanting to show solidarity, came to see the farmer and offered: "We are very sorry to hear your horse has run away. What terrible fortune!" Looking off into the distance where his horse had disappeared, the farmer responded: "Maybe."

The following morning, the sun rose to a surprising sight: Not only had the farmer's horse returned, but it had brought with it seven wild horses. Astonished by what they saw, the neighbors exclaimed, "You now have eight horses. What great luck!" The farmer again simply replied, "Maybe."

A day later, the farmer's son attempted to break one of the wild horses. But the horse bucked, causing the son to fall and break his leg. The neighbors came around and said, "That's such bad luck!" Again, the farmer said, "Maybe."

Then military officers arrived to draft young men for war. However, upon seeing the son's broken leg, they left the farmer's son behind. The neighbors shouted out: "Isn't that fantastic!" The farmer looked at the departing officers and answered, "Maybe."

Many are familiar with this parable, and yet we often struggle to accept change without judgment. One notable exception is former software developer Michael Singer. Singer had set out on a path that, with diligence and discipline, would lead him to a successful career as an economics professor. However, his plans didn't unfold as predicted.

After experiencing his own version of the farmer's "maybe"—several small crises yielding unexpected fruit—Singer resolved to take life as it came, accepting difficulties and opportunities without judging them through the lens of his ego. This attitude of nimble resilience paved the way to unexpected success, such as founding a groundbreaking software company, establishing a communal living center, and authoring several bestselling books.

Eventually, Singer faced what would have been, for many, a devastating crisis, when he was forced to resign as the CEO of his company following an FBI investigation that was ultimately dropped. During the investigation, he kept calm, navigating the lengthy legal process with grace and patience. When his name was cleared and still he had to hand over leadership of the company he had founded, he could have become bitter and fearful. Instead, he accepted the outcome, choosing to remain curious about the future rather than dwell on the past.

If giving in to life's whims without ever giving up can unlock doors we never knew existed, why do we struggle with remaining nimble in the face of disruption?

WHEN THINGS BREAK APART

Every day, you're confronted with unexpected events—someone says something you didn't see coming, you receive a phone call from a friend you don't talk to very often, you find money in a coat pocket, or there's a sudden change in weather. These gentle waves barely rock your boat; sometimes they require minor adjustments or even bring a bit of joy.

Disruptions, however, are a different beast. In Latin, *disruptus* means "to separate forcibly, to break apart." This gives us an insight into why disruptions feel so painful: they create a jarring gap between what we expect will happen and what does actually occur. These are the storms that test our mettle and force us to face how fragile our plans really are.

The stress caused by disruptions varies based on how much they force you to adapt. In other words, the degree to which you are forced to change defines the magnitude of a disruption. For this reason, even joyful occasions such as weddings and holidays can be experienced as disruptive—because of how drastically they alter the ordinary.

Disruptions may be especially upsetting when they interfere with important projects. The plans we lay and the roles we envision for ourselves give us a sense of control in the sea of chaos. Any disruption that derails these plans feels like more than just a change in direction: it's a direct attack on who we are and our place in the world. And the effects of this attack can be painful. Disruptive life events and personal stressors are associated with both anxiety and depression. In fact, a growing number of psychologists believe that disruptive life events play more of a role in someone's development of a mental illness than genetics do.

That's why, over thousands of years, philosophers and

spiritual leaders have advocated for a healthy form of letting go. Buddhism teaches that suffering arises from attachment to desires, including the desire for control over outcomes. Taoism talks about *wu wei,* which can be translated as "effortless action." This doesn't mean inaction but rather acting in harmony with the flow of life, without force or resistance. Similarly, in Hindu philosophy, *vairagya* is the detachment that allows us to experience greater levels of tranquility.

Western science is catching up to the Eastern spiritual teachings on the benefits of surrendering to the present moment and choosing to flow with the currents of life. Studies show that constantly trying to fight and fix the things that go wrong in life can lead to chronic stress, and that one of the hallmarks of psychological well-being is the ability to fluidly adapt to change—not to resist chaos, but embrace it.

Researchers distinguish between *active acceptance* and *resigning acceptance.* In both cases, people abandon fruitless attempts to control what they can't change. However, their mindset and outlook on life are different. "Active acceptance means acknowledging a negative, difficult situation and dealing with it in a constructive way," explain Yuka Maya Nakamura and Ulrich Orth from the University of Bern, Switzerland. "Resigning acceptance also means abandoning outward directed actions; however, this behavior is combined with negative expectations about the future and a loss of hope." Their research shows that only active acceptance is associated with better mental health, as people redirect their energy into more constructive actions to shape their lives.

Navigating life's disruptions isn't about completely abandoning hope, nor is it about blind tenacity—the positive can-do attitude some recommend maintaining in all circumstances. Instead, it calls for an in-between approach—an active embrace of life's inherent unpredictability. The key is to cultivate your own version of the farmer's "maybe."

Times of disruption are an opportunity to relax your grip on the outcome while you keep on showing up. Even in the face of adversity, we can send a powerful message to ourselves: our value isn't contingent upon perfect conditions or outcomes, but on our commitment to ourselves and our journey. Your role is to stick to your pact and allow the world to provide you with data. Just showing up—being an agent of change in a world that keeps on changing—can help you feel more confident in your ability to cope and more prepared to handle future setbacks.

As Vivian Greene puts it: "Life isn't about waiting for the storm to pass. It's about learning to dance in the rain." Accepting life's disruptions doesn't make you passive; it makes you agile.

THE TWO-STEP RESET

Disruptions inevitably interrupt our choreographed routines, but we can learn to dance with them. Finding your footing again is a two-step process, much like the two-step rhythmic pattern in various folk traditions. You must first explore the subjective experience with curiosity before calmly confronting the objective issues.

Although these two steps are not necessarily formalized in the way I will describe them below, you will find them in many schools of thought. Stoicism advocates, first and foremost, cultivating a state of calm regardless of external circumstances. Only then can you analyze situations logically to determine what's within your control and what's not. Many modern forms of therapy consist of recognizing unhelpful emotional responses that distort our belief systems and then, in a second phase, using that awareness to alter the corresponding maladaptive behaviors.

After years of inner work, Michael Singer arrived at the same conclusion: "I could see that the practice of surrender was actually done in two, very distinct steps: first, you let go of the personal reactions of like and dislike that form inside your mind and heart; and second, with the resultant sense of clarity, you simply look to see what is being asked of you by the situation unfolding in front of you."

STEP ONE: PROCESSING THE SUBJECTIVE EXPERIENCE

Disruption, by its very nature, shakes our emotional core. The first step is to pause and lean into these emotions. A rapid heart rate, a clenched jaw, shallow breathing, increased sweating, a sinking feeling in your stomach . . . Because the brain responds similarly to all threats, whether life-threatening or not, negative emotions that are not properly processed can impair our ability to evaluate situations, solve problems, and make decisions.

Uncomfortable emotions are not inherently bad. In the words of Emily Willroth, a psychologist at Washington University in St. Louis: "Anxiety can help you to face a potential threat, anger can help you stand up for yourself, and sadness can signal to other people that you need their social support." It's how we interpret our emotions that can cause suffering. You want to translate these bodily responses into a language your mind can assimilate.

For this, let's use a technique psychologists call affective labeling, which helps you better manage your physiological responses by naming your emotional states. Research has found that labeling our emotions results in higher brain activity in our prefrontal cortex, the part of the brain in charge of executive functioning, which, as we discussed in chapter 4, includes managing tasks, making decisions, and focusing attention. It also reduces activity in the amygdala, a region that plays an important role in emotional processing and the fight-or-flight response.

Affective labeling is literally "putting feelings into words." As you do this, vague anxieties crystallize into a clear set of solid emotions. The pioneer of writing therapy, James W. Pennebaker, explained that labeling our emotions relieves our brains of the burdensome task of processing them. Once you have those words, it's much easier to investigate their cause and address the issues underlying those feelings.

Suppose you're throwing a work event, and one of your suppliers is late with a delivery. Perhaps a client's last-minute cancellation causes your team to fall short of its quarterly quota. A workshop might have to be restructured because one of the speakers missed their flight. Maybe it's your flight that's canceled, and you cannot attend a conference to give a presentation.

Just ask yourself: *What am I feeling right now?* You don't even need to write complete sentences. Jotting down a list of adjectives that describe your emotions will do: for example, *tense, worried, nervous, uneasy, concerned.* You can do this in as little as five minutes. You can use a journal, a notes app, or a scrap of paper from the recycling bin. You can do it on walks by using the voice recorder on your phone, or through any medium that removes as much friction as possible between felt emotion and verbal expression.

If you're having trouble putting a name to a particular

emotion, you can use a proxy to describe how you feel. For instance, a long history of research has demonstrated that emotional states are closely related to landscapes. Landscapes seen as safe and resource-rich tend to elicit positive emotions. On the other hand, dense forests or extremely open deserts are perceived negatively, due to hidden dangers or a scarcity of resources. This effect is so strong that it persists in front of painted landscapes. You can leverage that primal connection to express your emotions in a more intuitive way. Maybe your feeling is a majestic but terrifying mountain, a vast and lonely ocean, a sandstorm over a desolate desert, or a big white cloud over the cliffs of a tiny beach town.

It's natural to experience some level of distress when faced with disruption. The best course of action is to process the emotion with curiosity and self-compassion so you can calmly deal with the consequences.

STEP TWO: MANAGING THE OBJECTIVE CONSEQUENCES

Once you have managed the emotional impact of the disruption, you can proceed to confront its practical implications. The repercussions of any event are akin to ripples in water. The disruption is evident at the point of impact, but its effect becomes more subtle as the waves spread out. To gracefully navigate these challenges, you must see beyond the obvious impact and into the more nuanced second-order consequences.

Scientists who study the effects of chain reactions—such as the spread of an epidemic or the domino effect of a power outage—call this a consequence cascade. To unravel the potential consequences of an event, they use computational models that analyze many what-if scenarios. The good news is you don't need to write complex programs. You can apply a simplified version of this method to deal with the objective problems that come up when something unexpected happens.

First, pinpoint the direct impact of the disruption by zeroing in on the most noticeable effects. Then map out potential consequences. This can be a quick list or a visual map. Think of this as the next wave emanating from the point of disruption. Then evaluate each potential consequence. Is it significant? Is it positive, negative, or neutral? Can it resolve on its own, or must something be done? Based on your assessment, you can decide whether to take action. You may choose to do nothing if the repercussions are minor or the issue will go away on its own. But if the problem is serious enough, it's worth putting some thought into how to fix it.

In the majority of cases, we have more agency than we think and can make smart decisions around when to pull the many levers at our disposal. Assessing the significance of a stressor can not only help reduce feelings of uncertainty and anxiety but also enhance your problem-solving abilities. It's a mental game of reacting but not overreacting, of defanging the fear and strategizing what response is required, if any.

This process might take only a few minutes if you quickly realize the consequences are negligible. Because you've already labeled and accepted your emotions as a natural reaction, you can cope with the minor disturbance and move on. Or it could take a couple of hours if you are dealing with a thorny issue linked to multiple orders of consequences.

Mapping all of these out will not necessarily solve all your problems, but it will help you go forward with more clarity and confidence in your ability to handle them or to surrender to the consequences.

AN ENDLESS WALTZ

New feelings may emerge as you progress through the layers of the consequence cascade. Some scenarios may cause fear and anxiety. If that's the case, simply go back to labeling those emotions and repeat the two-step reset—shifting between subjective experiences and objective consequences as many times as needed.

However, always err on the side of acceptance rather than control. Ride the wave of chaos instead of vainly trying to contain it. The point is not to create a master plan that gives you the illusion of power over the situation; rather, it is to de-escalate the consequences of any setback so you can move forward rather than give up.

Web developer Pierre Ntiruhungwa expected some disruption when he quit his job to launch a company. But a few months into the process, his cofounder experienced health issues and they were forced to place the venture on hold. Faced with the financial implications of this unexpected crisis, Ntiruhungwa found that his mindful productivity systems all went out the window. "I started saying yes to everything to not be in a position where I don't have money—even jobs that paid really low just so I could pay rent. I was working a lot, including the unpaid job of trying to find jobs."

To navigate the disruption and come back to a place of active acceptance, Ntiruhungwa first labeled his emotions: the shaken confidence, the insecurity, the helplessness. Although the uncertainty was still there, he knew these subjective experiences were valid and was then able to calmly tackle the objective repercussions. He asked a few friends to lend him some money to make rent, which allowed him to be more selective with clients and to build strong relationships with several web development agencies. His freelance business is now thriving, but he still occasionally faces disruptions—at which point he can simply repeat the two-step reset.

Once you learn to cultivate the resolute determination to let go, not only will you feel less stressed in the face of disruption, but you'll be able to better navigate it. As philosopher Alan Watts once said of life, "It was a musical thing, and you were supposed to sing or to dance while the music was being played." Life, like music, carries highs and lows, crescendos and silences. Embracing these movements is not just a strategy—it's the very essence of the dance. The tumult of change can catalyze fresh ideas. New opportunities arise through the ups and downs. It's a vast, dynamic ecosystem that invites you to engage in creative problem-solving.

Waltzing with chaos isn't just about survival—it's about feeling alive and open to the world, welcoming change as a source of growth, and finding humor in life's trickiest moments.

IMPACT

Grow with the World

10

How to Unlock Social Flow

My newsletter always ends with a postscriptum, where I share a simple question, usually asking readers how they are doing and encouraging self-reflection. In March 2020, as the COVID-19 pandemic lockdowns began, hundreds of answers poured in—many more than usual. "I'm feeling disconnected," "Work is lonely," "I'm in a creative rut," "I'm anxious about the future," they read. The lockdowns were an acute demonstration of what happens when we are cut off from the generative energy of our peers. Our mental health suffers, our focus dissipates, our inspiration dwindles.

While individual curiosity can produce incredible feats, our collective curiosity is the motor behind humanity's biggest innovations. Conversations feed our imagination and collaboration enables us to dream bigger. In fact, we are wired to function at our best when tapping into shared knowledge and the support of a community.

You've probably heard of the concept of flow states, which I briefly mentioned in chapter 4—those moments when you feel completely focused and engaged while working or playing.

But much of the attention on these states has been on solitary activities, such as playing the violin or writing poetry.

However, researchers have found that flow states happen more easily in group activities than in solitary ones. Chamber music players are more likely to report being "in the zone" during small group performances than when practicing alone. In sports such as rowing and football, athletes can more readily experience personal flow states during collaborative play, even though their teammates may not necessarily be in flow. The interdependent nature of these sports improves the focus of each individual. And even though solitary flow is quite enjoyable, studies have found that the intrinsic reward of shared focus alongside others makes sinking into that optimal state even more pleasurable.

When you experience social flow, the energy of the group invigorates your own thinking and the shared focus sharpens your concentration. The group's flow pulls you deeper into your process. Beyond the increased focus, gatherings produce a profound sense of fulfillment. Social flow enhances not only the end result but the experience of getting there.

The rewarding experience of social flow is why many of the most influential artists, philosophers, and scientists have actively participated in vibrant "scenes"—creative communities where like-minded individuals exchange ideas and inspire one another.

Impressionist painters in nineteenth-century Paris gathered in cafés to debate artistic techniques. This scene gave Monet and Renoir access to new ideas about color and light, which they incorporated into their revolutionary painting style. In Vienna, salons provided Freud with insights that helped shape his theories of psychoanalysis. The legendary discussions at the Algonquin Round Table in New York brought together writers, critics, and actors, sparking witty exchanges that not only honed their individual crafts but also profoundly influenced American literature and drama. The Bloomsbury Group formed an intellectual and artistic scene in early twentieth-century London, where Virginia Woolf exchanged ideas with peers such as John Maynard Keynes and E. M. Forster.

Throughout history, such hubs have provided fertile ground for creative and intellectual growth. "It's much easier to hold a thought during a salon, even for hours and hours, than just think about it by yourself," explained Anna Gát, who is reviving the nineteenth-century salon with Interintellect, a community designed around thoughtful and considerate conversations. "The salons create an experience of shared humanity. We can co-think together, in conversation." By unlocking the power of social flow, Interintellect members have written books together, started companies, quit jobs, or even moved countries because they were inspired by this global network.

Social flow, or at least the footprint left by it, even translates to value in the art world. What collectors call the provenance of a work—the context in which a piece is created, the story around it, the people who were interested in it and owned it: in essence, whose lives the work has touched—matters hugely to its valuation.

When you surround yourself with people who encourage you to experiment and grow, you will unlock new communities of practice and creative territories you couldn't have discovered on your own. Instead of being the result of solitary thinking, your ideas become woven into a narrative that people want to be a part of.

POWER IN COMMUNITY

Across history, many schools of thought converged on this singular truth: none of us can flourish on our own. But our cultural narrative continues to romanticize the lone hero. For example, the story of Einstein's $E = mc^2$ as an isolated breakthrough fails to acknowledge the foundational contributions of scientists such as French mathematician and theoretical physicist Henri Poincaré, who previously discussed the relativity of space and formulated an equation remarkably similar to Einstein's: the less well known $m = E/c^2$. Alongside Poincaré, Dutch physicist Hendrik Lorentz also provided critical theoretical insights that paved the way for Einstein's breakthrough.

Each of these individuals contributed pieces to a puzzle that no one person could have solved alone. Social flow helps explain why *what* you know is inseparable from *who* you know. Instead of feeling like building relationships is the "dirty work" of your otherwise exciting experiments—the grim but necessary self-promotion that distracts you from making progress and honing your craft—you will find that the relationships worth prioritizing won't distract from your work at all. They'll improve your work. They'll support your work. They'll inspire new work.

By compounding individual curiosity, social flow has three powerful effects—and it's these that make a community uniquely valuable, much more so than its members' status or strategic influence.

THE POOLING EFFECT

A community will give you access to a collective set of knowledge, skills, and physical assets that vastly exceed your own.

Those communal resources empower you not only to achieve things you could not do independently, but to do so more efficiently. This way, your network's diverse expertise and talents will complement your own abilities to expand your potential.

Psychologists call this transactive memory, a system where individuals develop an understanding of who knows what, enabling them to leverage the group's knowledge and make progress more effectively.

Marathon runners can concentrate on running faster, knowing their coach handles training, their nutritionist plans the optimal diet, and their sponsor facilitates the logistics. Chefs craft exquisite dishes, relying on their teams to handle kitchen operations. In the high-stakes setting of an emergency room, doctors count on the specialized knowledge and skills of nurses, technicians, and other specialists, so they can save more lives by focusing on urgent diagnoses. By tapping into the group mind, you can enhance your own efficiency and reach. You save time and energy by focusing on your areas of specialty, trusting group members to fill knowledge gaps.

That's why Courtland Allen started Indie Hackers: to create a community where people could pool knowledge and resources to help one another build online businesses. He saw a need for aspiring founders to have access to practical advice and stories from others who had built successful independent companies—not the polished press releases we see in magazines, but the tactics and strategies, the revenue numbers, the real challenges faced by founders. By bringing this community together, he aimed to make that invaluable information more accessible so he and other people could learn from others' experiences.

His work resonated with others: less than a year after the launch of the community, it was acquired by Stripe, and Allen's brother, Channing, joined as a cofounder. Indie Hackers has become a vibrant platform with thousands of founders sharing their journeys, asking questions, and exchanging ideas. "Whatever the path you want to take in entrepreneurship, there is someone like you on Indie Hackers who has shared their story," said Channing. "You can say, *Here's what I am like and here's the kind of business I want to build*. And then you can find people who are just like you who have shared their advice transparently."

As an active participant in a community, you gain access to a living repository of collective knowledge that cannot be replicated in static resources. That's why people turn to forums such as Reddit and Quora for specific, timely questions instead of sifting through a magazine or a book. "The good thing about a community is that people talk—a lot," said Courtland. "Through those interactions, it creates something that's more than the sum of its parts." These communities facilitate an ongoing exchange of new ideas and best practices, keeping you informed as the world changes and allowing you to put questions directly to the community.

In fact, researchers found that information exchange is the most popular reason for joining a community. The specialized, up-to-the-minute information and support from these collaborative platforms provide an edge over those still relying on conventional one-way information sources. Tapping into collective curiosity almost becomes an unfair advantage.

THE RIPPLE EFFECT

If you participate with genuine curiosity, a community can impact your path in unexpected ways. You join with a specific benefit in mind, but the relationships that flourish unlock opportunities that might have once seemed outside of the realm of possible. A writer might meet a developer, and together they start a profitable startup. A student might connect with an industry veteran who becomes their mentor. You may discover new interests or business ideas. The people you meet can become collaborators, clients, employers, or advisors.

Such interactions are especially likely in what researchers call communities of practice—groups of people who genuinely care about the same issues and frequently engage to learn from one another. For instance, people tend to join the Ness Labs community to share mindful productivity advice. But over the years, I have heard about community members who have started businesses together, co-created workshops and online courses, found freelance work, or hired members of the community.

Andrew Nalband, founder of note-taking app Thunk, found several collaborators in the community: "Through Ness Labs, a developer offered to help me with front-end work, and she ended up working part time with me for a while. A lot of my early Thunk users actually came from Ness Labs, because it was a place where you could share what you were working on. I also ended up creating a writing course with another member."

Some became language-learning partners: "We are both entrepreneurs who are interested in productivity, so the flash cards I create after receiving feedback on our weekly chat are easier to remember, as they're on topics that mean something to me," designer and educational publisher Ellane Weedon told me.

For IT specialist Lukas Rosenstock, the community has offered a platform to discuss books and create accountability. "Such a community provides a way to kick-start things because you know you'll find people who'd be interested in joining," he explained. It has also unexpectedly changed the way he travels. Now when he goes somewhere new, he traces an itinerary based on the people he would like to meet in person. "I'm visiting cities where I've never been, but it feels like coming back to meet friends." This applies to when people visit his country as well. "There was a person from India that I first met in the Ness Labs community, and when she traveled to Germany, she reached out to me and stayed at my house for a day. We noticed that there was a lot of trust. She said that it was because we were part of the same circles, the same professional community. Because we had some common connections, it didn't feel like meeting a stranger."

The ripple effect can profoundly shape your journey in unanticipated ways. By being open to serendipitous opportunities, you can gain fresh perspectives, forge meaningful relationships, and grow beyond your initial expectations.

THE SAFETY EFFECT

It's harder to stay curious when your life is unstable. Communities can provide critical help when you are navigating new or difficult situations. They offer emotional support, advice, and a sense of belonging, all of which help you stay resilient when facing challenges in your personal or professional life. That's why studies suggest that being part of a community improves your mental health and happiness.

When you lose a job, members can connect you with new opportunities. If you face a legal issue, someone may offer advisor referrals. When a family member passes away, a community can raise money to cover expenses. Beyond practical help, a community can also provide moral support. UX designer Tamara Sredojevic felt supported by the members of the Women Make community while transitioning her career from marketing to web design. "We exchanged tips on the best online courses. Members offered their expert feedback when I released my first portfolio; others offered to give me a hand with the code on my websites. I also got to know people who coached me on progressing my career, as well as people who I later recruited to work with me on bigger projects."

She credits the spirit of collaboration rather than competition between the women in this community for creating a safe space where she could discuss important issues such as inclusion, diversity, ethical design, and accessibility, which later became her specialty. "I owe these women a lot," she says.

DON'T THINK THAT all your needs have to be met by one single group. Our needs for community are multifaceted. A local mastermind can offer peer support and accountability, a recreational sports team can provide excitement over a shared challenge, and a local nonprofit can let you contribute your skills to a cause you care about. An online forum can help you stay on top of industry trends, while your college alumni group provides opportunities for networking and professional development.

Beyond the practical benefits of drawing on your peers' intellectual and creative energy, the bonds you form will provide a sense of belonging, making the journey more enjoyable. By supporting and uplifting those around you, you will enrich your own life.

TAPPING INTO COLLECTIVE CURIOSITY

Attending events where you don't know anyone, spearheading a group effort, or putting yourself out there to mentor others are big steps outside most people's comfort zones. You may worry you won't have enough time or energy to commit or that you will be expected to do more than you're able to give. However, communities do not have to be overwhelming. You decide your level of involvement. You can start small and progressively ramp up your commitment to collective curiosity.

- **The Apprentice.** If plunging into a new community seems daunting, start by being more intentional about your existing relationships. You can start by curating your community with care. Choose to invest in fewer relationships through deeper conversations, share your authentic self, ask thoughtful questions, and listen closely to understand the perspectives of others. Consider where you can find people who share similar interests. You could join a book club, attend local events, or reach out to old connections you have lost touch with.

- **The Artisan.** When you feel ready for more involvement, you can start actively applying your skills to contribute to the community. Look for ways to help others along their journey, whether it's giving advice to someone just starting out, collaborating with peers on projects, volunteering to speak at an event, or writing a guest blog post. In the Ness Labs community, hundreds of workshops have been hosted by volunteers who wanted to give back. For instance, health coach Javier Luis Gomez has been hosting weekly coworking sessions for fellow members. "The more you put into a community, the more you get out of it," he explained. "I get stuff done, and it's nice to get to see the same people week after week, to have this sense that there are people out there who know my story." The key is to figure out how your own curiosity might serve others.

- **The Architect.** Eventually you may feel called to scale up your impact by shaping the vision and structure of the community or maybe even building your own community. There are many ways to become a community architect. The Rebel Book Club started when two friends, Ben Keene and Ben Saul-Garner, committed to reading one book together every month and then decided to invite other people to join in. A hundred books later, the community has grown to thousands of members. Derrick Downey Jr. started posting videos of the squirrels visiting him on his patio and has now built an unlikely global community of squirrel lovers who share tips and snack ideas in his comments section. And the Ness Labs community sprouted out of the newsletter when I transitioned from a one-way broadcasting relationship to acting as a facilitator, providing a platform for people to connect and learn from one another.

BECOMING THE ARCHITECT

Anyone can turn their curiosity into a thriving community. You don't have to be a savant or even particularly charismatic. You just need to assemble a circle of fellow curious minds who would like to explore similar ideas together.

What I like to call a curiosity circle is a community centered around genuine connection and peer learning. It could be around a common interest or a shared experience, and eligibility to join should not be based on expertise but on curiosity.

Building a curiosity circle is less like lighting a match and more like building a campfire. Your community will not survive—and you will not survive it—if it has to rely on your fuel alone for very long. I've myself led several such communities of all sizes at various stages of my life, including the largest online community for young writers in France; a small community of newsletter writers; and of course, the Ness Labs community. The following are the lessons I've learned along the way.

Start scrappy. *Jugaad*, a Hindi term for innovative problem-solving using limited resources, emphasizes starting small and creatively using what's available. It's considered a form of frugal engineering, allowing you to start something new without needing extensive resources. Instead of picturing large weekly meetups with catering and speakers, ask yourself: What would be the smallest, easiest version of a curiosity circle you could bring to life with your current resources? After building Tea with Strangers, a community of fifty thousand members in twenty-five cities coming together for meaningful conversations over tea, Ankit Shah knows a thing or two about running a large community. And yet when he wanted to connect with other people around his meditation practice, he decided to start a small meditation circle in his living room with just a few cushions and candles. "Starting big can get in the way of finding your people. When I think of bringing people together for any kind of community gathering, I think of what I'm actually looking for," he told me. "I wanted to meditate once a week in a group. This does not require me to build a big meditation organization." Your curiosity circle may grow organically, or it may feel just right as a small group. Let those decisions emerge along the way.

Be up front. When Lukas Rosenstock hosted his first after-work party at his home, he embraced not having it figured all out. "I didn't pretend to be confident about the concept, but instead always mentioned that I got the idea from a book and that it was an experiment, so people knew what they signed up for," he explained. Studies suggest that we form deeper relationships through self-disclosure—when we share vulnerable information such as our motives, desires, and worries. By being open about the experimental nature of your community, you encourage others to be open, too. Whether you start a community for the first or the tenth time, tell people that you are learning as you go and that you might make mistakes. This way, your curiosity circle becomes a space for co-exploration, where everyone shapes the experience.

Don't overthink it. People who are action-oriented tend to thrive in new or unfamiliar environments, as they quickly take initiative rather than getting stuck in indecision. This kind of proactive approach is especially beneficial when creating a curiosity circle. When he moved with his partner from London to Folkestone, a seaside town in South East England, Carl Martin immediately felt at home. He loved the cute main street with artsy shops and the easy access to nature. And because he was working remotely, he relished the quiet of his home office. The couple settled down into a nice routine, with the occasional visits from friends and family. However, as he was about to become a dad, Martin felt the need to connect and learn from other men. Instead of overthinking it, he posted a simple notice online: "Men of Folkestone, how would you like a space to meet other lads and dads, chat about life, manhood and make friends?" More than twenty people came to the first meetup. "Afterwards someone said, 'You have no idea how much I needed this,'" Martin told me. "It's just the simplicity of feeling connected to someone." This bias for action paid off. Today there are more than a hundred men in the Folkstone Fellas group chat.

Make it cozy. Fostering psychological safety, where members feel they can speak up without risk of being punished or judged, is key to making your curiosity circle secure and inclusive. "A lot of the advice I give first-time hosts is to let their guests know what to expect," Nick Gray, author of *The 2-Hour Cocktail Party*, told me. "Especially for introverts or people with social anxiety, that will help with psychological safety." The same goes for new members of your community. A few signposts can ensure everyone is at ease. Depending on the format, this could be as simple as listing potential topics of conversation and, if it's in person, the kinds of snacks and facilities that will be available. This creates ambient belonging, where individuals sense they fit in and are welcome. When people feel at home, they are more likely to participate fully, share openly, and engage deeply. Being comfortable also makes it easier for members to have honest, meaningful conversations—even, and maybe especially, when they disagree. As Adam Grant puts it, "The clearest sign of intellectual chemistry isn't agreeing with someone. It's enjoying your disagreements with them."

Don't hold the reins too tight. While having a vision is important, too much structure can stifle spontaneity and creativity. Giving members freedom to take the initiative can lead to unexpected manifestations of collective curiosity, and embracing distributed leadership, where responsibilities are shared among group members, promotes collaboration and shared decision-making. Rosie Sherry has run local meetups, a coworking space, and several online communities. Today she advises companies on community building. "As community builders, it's our responsibility to lift members up and show people they have good ideas." Encourage autonomy, competence, and relatedness—key aspects of self-determination—and allow for informal interactions and unplanned activities, as these can foster interesting ideas and connections. At Ness Labs, we let members self-organize support groups around topics they care about, and we have members who host their own recurring events in the community. This approach has led to the creation of a group for writers and a group for neurodivergent community members, among many others, which I would not have had the idea or the resources to launch myself.

The journey to collective curiosity does not have to be overwhelming. Start with small steps that feel comfortable. Intentionally nurture your existing relationships. Contribute your skills and experiences to communities you already belong to. Move at your own pace, listen to your needs, and incrementally make the commitments that fit this season of your life.

Before long, you will look around to see a tribe that fosters social flow and supports you—fellow curious minds who expand your horizons, amplify your impact, and provide safety as you navigate the bumps and swerves of an experimental life.

☷ *Learning in Public*

The astronomer Galileo changed humankind's understanding of the world forever. On the morning of July 25, 1610, he pointed his telescope at Saturn and observed that it wasn't just a single object. Instead, alongside Saturn's sphere, he saw two small dots—the first ever hint of its now-famous rings. Galileo immediately sent out letters to his colleagues, but instead of clearly stating what he'd just observed, he described his discovery in the form of an anagram:

smaismrmilmepoetaleumibunenugttauiras

. . . which stands for *Altissimum planetam tergeminum observavi* ("I have observed the most distant planet to have a triple form"). By using an anagram, he avoided prematurely revealing any details and ensured that if someone else—such as his great rival Johannes Kepler—later made the same discovery, Galileo could reveal the anagram and claim the credit. The anagram bought him time so he could independently build upon the discovery. Kepler himself, Isaac Newton,

Christiaan Huygens, and Robert Hooke, and many other scientists used similar devices to "patent" their discoveries.

Compare this secrecy to what happened almost four hundred years later, on January 27, 2009, when a mathematician named Tim Gowers used his blog to run a public experiment. A recipient of the Fields Medal, the highest honor in mathematics, Gowers is not just any mathematician. And yet he was struggling to solve a problem. Instead of wrestling with it alone, he invited the community to contribute ideas through the comments section of his blog—a radical departure from the traditional solitary approach to research in mathematics. He called this experiment the Polymath Project.

In the next month or so, twenty-seven mathematicians submitted more than eight hundred comments. As quantum physicist Michael Nielsen remarked in a talk he gave at the Carnegie Council: "That's a lot of mathematics very quickly." Only thirty-seven days after the launch of the experiment, Gowers announced that not only was the original problem solved, but that a harder mathematical problem that included the original as a special case had been solved as well. "This has been one of the most exciting six weeks of my mathematical life," he said. He went on to initiate several more Polymath Projects on various unsolved problems, pioneering a model of transparent inquiry in his community and further establishing himself at the forefront of open and collaborative mathematics.

Gowers and other members of the open science movement embody a spirit of public exploration. Rather than shield their work until they can share a polished final product, they openly document the meandering process, missteps and all, and invite fellow explorers to join their quest. What unites these scientists is the courage to learn in public. This act of radical transparency allows others to build on their embryonic ideas much faster and for everyone to grow together.

The spirit of learning in public applies not just to mathematics. When you become the scientist of your own life, sharing your experiments along the way provides fuel for your personal growth, leading to fresh discoveries and improving your rate of success.

When Karthik Puvvada, who goes by KP, moved from India to the United States as a graduate student and teaching assistant, he knew this was where he wanted to build his life. He also knew navigating the immigration system would require patience and proof of his work contributions.

For ten years, KP worked in corporate jobs to maintain a visa while preparing for the time he hoped he'd be allowed to run his own startup. And he shared everything he learned in the process. When he studied how to build an audience on Twitter, he created a Twitter beginner's guide. When he taught himself how to use AI tools, he published a list of his favorites. After conducting several cold emailing experiments, he fine tuned the best template for getting a response and shared it on his website.

"I was learning so much, I wanted to make sure anyone who would come after would have it easier than me," he told me. "I also believe that to become better at something, you need to apply it but also to teach it."

More recently, KP made a pact of conducting interviews with successful founders every week and sharing the lessons with the world. This project allowed him to learn directly from the likes of Alexis Ohanian (founder of Reddit), Kat Cole (president of Athletic Greens), Sahil Lavingia (founder of Gumroad), and Gary Vaynerchuk (founder of VaynerMedia and cofounder of Resy). "If you're genuinely curious and you want to learn from them, most of the world's top experts want to share their knowledge because they're very curious themselves. So if you go at it from an angle of curiosity and willingness to learn, and ask them interesting questions, they're likely to give you a shot and teach you something."

Since moving to the United States, he has now obtained his green card and launched his own startup. "This has given me a shot in the global arena. Now if I want to change jobs or if I'm looking for some feedback or any distribution help, I have this amazing network of people who are willing to provide support because they trust me," he explained. "There is no doubt I will keep on building my career and my projects in public for the next decades."

By the time I sent the very first Ness Labs newsletter in the summer of 2019, the open science movement had made ripples outside of academia. Founders were gathering around the open startup movement, a group of companies embracing transparency by sharing their progress and insights with everyone. Some simply shared screenshots of their latest metrics, while others built live dashboards and published blog posts with all the lessons they learned on their entrepreneurial journey. I was inspired by the energy and generosity of this community, and I decided that I would learn in public—openly sharing my progress as I grew both Ness Labs as a business and myself as a researcher and entrepreneur.

The open startup movement was in its infancy and there was no step-by-step manual to follow, but I shared early drafts and milestones and asked a lot of questions. What tool was best for managing a newsletter? Where should I promote my articles? How could I optimize my website for search engines? I experimented with the recommendations I received and then shared the results, creating a public cycle of experimentation anyone was welcome to join.

STEPPING INTO THE ARENA

In ancient Greece, learning in public was woven into everyday life. To acquire new knowledge, you ventured into the bustling agora, the public square. There, elders shared their wisdom with small crowds, and you could join animated debates between scholars. To propose a new philosophical theory, you presented it openly in the polis, subjecting it to public scrutiny and critique. This offered the chance to refine ideas, but also the risk of public shame if your logic proved faulty. Beyond political debates, tradespeople peddled new business ideas and products. Inventors demonstrated prototypes, inviting feedback. Progress came not just from solitary thought but from the creative friction of diverse viewpoints colliding.

Today there is no well-defined universal public arena to grow and learn in. Forums are fragmented and often online, with opaque and ever-shifting social codes.

How much of your process should you share publicly, and where? With whom should you share—friends, colleagues, your wider community? How often should you share and how often is too often, straying into oversharing?

Conducting a personal experiment *in public* offers an opportunity to answer these questions for yourself. Your pact is a perfect means of stepping into the arena. It's a starting place to practice the art of learning in public, with all its joys and understandable fears.

In chapter 8, I mentioned my successful meditation pact,

and how I had to resist the temptation to scale it up. I didn't share the details of *why* I was able to be successful with it, when I had failed to stick to meditation in the past.

Previous attempts had looked something like this: installing an app to follow a ten-day guided program, each day fidgeting and waiting uncomfortably for the torture to be over, and ultimately finding excuses—too busy, too tired—to abandon the attempt somewhere around day three.

When I finally decided to create a formal pact, I did something new: I opted to run the experiment in public. I created an online document, shared it around—including with a few seasoned meditators I knew—and committed to writing notes in that document after each meditation session. This was my vow of radical transparency—a public pledge to share every up and down along the way.

The public platform I chose was a simple online document that allowed for active collaboration. My friends left many helpful comments. Regarding the fifteen-minute length, writer and engineer Bryan Kam commented: "This is a long sit for an absolute beginner! Just as an FYI. If you can do it, that's amazing, though. You'll progress fast with that." Breathwork specialist Jonny Miller recommended starting with a few minutes of breathing "to calm the monkey mind." When I complained that I was distracted by business ideas, project manager Sailesh Raithatha said, "This happens to me often, too—best to write them down and then continue where you left off!"

Receiving advice and assurances that my experience was typical helped me a great deal in sticking to my pact while continuously iterating. Each day, I tweaked my approach based on the feedback I received the previous day. A quick body scan at the beginning of the session seemed to help;

meditating with my eyes open did not. Slowly I began to understand what people meant when they said, "You are not your thoughts," even though I could tell that it'd take a lot more practice to embody this principle, that maybe I would never get there, and that was fine.

Then one morning something incredible happened: I rushed to get up earlier so I'd manage to fit in my meditation session before I had to go to the airport. Somewhere along the way, I had started looking forward to the practice, and I didn't want to miss it!

Since then, meditation has become a habit. It's an imperfect one—now that nobody's watching, I sometimes miss a day or two—but it's become part of my ideal routine. I notice when I haven't meditated, and I no longer believe that meditation isn't working for me.

If, like me, there is an experiment you've tried a few times without success but believe could positively impact your life were you to complete it, here is how to use the three Public Pillars—public pledge, public platform, public practice—to share your learning journey.

1. MAKE A PLEDGE

You've already learned how to design a pact to turn your doubts into experiments. You can add a layer of accountability and support by making a public pledge. When we make our ambitions known to others, we feel a greater sense of responsibility to follow through. A public pledge acts as a form of commitment device, increasing the likelihood of maintaining your efforts.

Start by defining who you will share your learning journey with. Will it be colleagues and peers? Fellow members of a local community? Or a more general audience? Both niche and broad groups offer distinct benefits and challenges. Intimate groups provide more depth and privacy but can turn into echo chambers. Broader communities include more diverse perspectives but lack the safety and trust of close collaborators.

When choosing who to share your pact with, ask yourself: *Will they support my learning journey or foster unhealthy comparison?* Seek supportive team players who can share constructive feedback with empathy.

Then comes the simplest but not necessarily easiest part: tell them about your experiment and the pact you are committing to. Write a text or a tweet, take a deep breath, and hit send. Voilà—you have announced your experiment to the world. Now, however, you need to follow through: to conduct the entire experiment in public, including documenting everything you learn and the tweaks you make along the way. Studies have shown that announcing a goal has the unfortunate effect of making you less likely to complete it. Making a pledge to conduct your experiment in public helps ensure that you don't drop your pact after the dopamine hit from announcing it.

2. CHOOSE A PLATFORM

People will need a way to follow your progress so they can support you. The right platform aligns with your project's nature and feels easy to navigate. Research shows that choosing a familiar platform can increase its perceived usefulness, making it more likely that you will use it effectively and consistently. Avoid using new tools or entering new spaces that require deciphering opaque norms while simultaneously trying to complete your pact.

When Danny Miranda made the ambitious pact of publishing three podcast episodes per week, he decided to use Twitter to document his process, such as how he reached out to guests and prepared for the interviews. "I'm trying to show the human side of producing the podcast. I'm sharing what's happening, what I'm struggling with," he said. "I love getting help and receiving help, and I still often underestimate the help that people are willing to give." Learning in public has led to a burgeoning community and a lot of support. People have provided strategic advice, introduced him to prominent guests, and even redesigned his landing page for free.

Like Miranda, resist spreading yourself thin when choosing a public platform. Ground yourself in one space that feels like home so that you can focus wholly on your learning journey. It can be as simple as an online document, a private group chat, or a short newsletter. Once you have developed your voice and approach to learning in public, expand organically to new platforms if connecting with a wider community is something you want.

3. PRACTICE AND ITERATE

Once you've made your pledge and chosen your platform, you just need to run your experiment while documenting what you learn along the way and tweaking your approach as you go, based on the feedback you receive.

Just as in the gym, start small to build confidence. This will enhance your belief in your ability to succeed, which is crucial for learning in public. As you become more comfortable, move toward sharing some of your more ambitious work-in-progress projects and ideas.

Artist Lois van Baarle, who goes by Loish, regularly posted sketches online before progressively sharing more insights into her creative process through art books, lectures, and even live demonstrations. Biochemist Dr. Rhonda Patrick first published scientific papers read only by her fellow academics, and then started publicly sharing about her personal diet and how it aligns with current scientific understanding in the field of nutrition and wellness. Author of fantasy and science fiction Brandon Sanderson began by sharing advice on his personal website, before expanding to live streaming Q&As about his work, even allowing people to watch him write.

In my case, I started with simply sharing short notes after each meditation, but as I became more comfortable, I shared more detailed notes and short videos of how I was trying different techniques, various postures, and even one longer thirty-minute meditation.

The way you share your learning journey can also evolve over time. You may want to share a weekly note with your team about what you learned that week, before putting together a monthly co-learning meeting. An entrepreneur might first share business books they enjoyed before revealing their own startup ideas. An artist could post their sources of inspiration before they start sharing original sketches. Expand the spotlight at your own pace.

HOW TO EMBRACE RADICAL TRANSPARENCY

After trying kombucha in Sri Lanka, Eaoifa Forward wanted to find the fermented drink at home in England. Nothing she could find matched the flavor. She decided to create her own kombucha using only traditional Far Eastern methods, taking over her tiny kitchen and spare room in a high-rise building in London. When I first met her several years ago as a plus-one at her birthday party, she greeted me warmly, then put a little glass bottle in my hand. "Tell me what you think," she said. In her birthday speech, she asked everyone to try the samples on the tables and to share their feedback.

Learning in public requires connecting with other humans to explore, learn, and grow together. It's a form of iterative learning, where mistakes and errors are valuable opportunities for improvement. As such, it is messy. When I asked about her process, Forward said she did a lot of taste testing: "I went to farmers' markets every weekend." Only five years later, she has graduated from personal deliveries to her friends to pallets of boxes sent to a wholesaler, which then dispatches her kombucha to retailers all around the country. She now owns a 1,000-square-foot unit with a temperature-controlled brew room equipped with a lidding machine and a bottle labeler.

By nature, experiments are imperfect. They can also be a bit scary. However, iterating in public creates a culture of learning around yourself. A scholar might blog about their research to get real-time feedback from peers. A startup founder might build a scrappy version of their product to gauge demand. A designer could publish rough sketches. In each case, putting forward unpolished ideas sparks an ongoing dialogue, to reveal any gaps and iterate rapidly.

Podcast host Steph Smith has a page on her website where she shares the number of days she has exercised throughout the year, the books she is reading, the online courses she is taking, the side projects she is working on, and even the revenue these projects are generating. "I wanted to create a transparent place for myself to share my progress and for other people to get to see what I was doing," she told me. "It was a way of opening myself up as a person to people, so they could see what I'm working on and the nuances of what I'm interested in."

She also stresses the importance of sharing both the highs and the lows, which means updating her page even when she falls short of her ambitions. For instance, she tried several times to achieve specific exercise targets. "I don't think I hit them in any of the three years. So you can see that transparently." This is an extreme form of vulnerability, which has been found to foster a deeper sense of connection, trust, and empathy. And the sense of accountability gained by going public allowed her to get further than she would have if she had pursued these and other targets in secrecy.

Her candor has struck a chord. "This is one of the pages that I get emails about the most," she said. "I'm constantly surprised by the little things that people resonate with." People ask her about the books she has read, her exercise routine, the online courses she took. In a sea of dry information, her openness offers a reminder that behind the work there is a human, one who welcomes connection.

Growth often comes from struggle, frustration, confusion—but we usually keep those moments private for fear of being exposed as a "fraud." We worry that others will judge us as unqualified despite these being common experiences in the learning process. Learning in public is the opposite of pretending you have everything figured out. Instead, share your real work in real time—the raw stuff, not the highlights reel.

Open your notebook to show all the crossed-out ideas, half-baked drafts, and scribbled margins. Share your evolving fitness regimens, journaling techniques, or any ongoing experiment. If you work at a company, prototype publicly, encourage product development teams to solicit early customer feedback, and convey challenges openly. When studying something new—for example, a new language or a new software—pull back the curtain on the learning process by sharing your questions, mistakes, and insights throughout the journey. Share even the lessons from an experiment that failed.

To do all this, you'll need to become comfortable saying *I don't know* and asking others for input. Ultimately, learning in public strengthens your thinking by exposing your ideas to diverse perspectives early on. This can save you precious time and money. It also builds public trust and engagement by letting your stakeholders—whether colleagues or customers— witness firsthand the discovery process, with all its ups and downs.

Above all, welcome new inputs instead of just promoting your own point of view. As Gowers remarked when reflecting on the Polymath Project, what he found most striking was "how often I found myself having thoughts that I would not have had without some chance remark of another contributor." By working together, progress compounds exponentially.

Learn the art of give-and-take—listening as much as sharing, valuing diverse voices, and recognizing each contribution, however small. When you learn in public, you create an open playbook welcoming new players to advance the game beyond what you first imagined, sparking new connections, sharing both the credit and the challenges.

This is how Pieter Levels created Nomad List, a platform to discover the best places to live for digital nomads. Nomad List began as a modest spreadsheet that Levels made public to crowdsource data from Twitter in 2014. People added the data he requested, but then went further, adding columns for indicators such as level of safety, LGBTQ-friendliness, and coffee shop density. "I was slightly stunned by the response," he said. Based on the data, he quickly put together a minimally viable version of the Nomad List platform, documenting the process in public. That early prototype drew enthusiastic notice in *Forbes, Lifehacker, Business Insider,* and many more press outlets; even Tim Ferriss shared it with his audience.

When Levels wondered how he might monetize all the attention, he simply asked Nomad List's users for ideas. The request received over four hundred answers and more than fifty people directly replied to his email. Today Nomad List brings in about $700,000 in annual revenue—and Levels is still an independent solopreneur. "How did I do this?" he asks. "By building it while actively listening to user feedback and being completely open about it."

Learning in public unlocks powerful mechanisms to support your personal and professional growth:

- **Get early feedback.** Sharing your work in public ensures that what you are working on answering an actual need and allows you to take a more iterative approach.

- **Increase your creativity.** By publishing your work in progress, you will increase the likelihood that you will connect the dots between your ideas and other people's ideas.

- **Clarify your thinking.** Instead of just plowing through work, you will be nudged to think about your strategy and execution in a deeper way—another opportunity to practice metacognition.

- **Build your network.** Learning in public is a great way to connect with people who are interested in a similar space. It may result in finding a mentor or lead to partnerships.

- **Learn faster.** By documenting your progress openly, including your challenges and questions, you can connect with others who have expertise and can suggest resources to build your skills more efficiently.

Most significant breakthroughs, from the printing press to vaccinations, resulted from the combined efforts of many people building knowledge across vast networks of minds. Learning in public can fast-forward your progress—but it requires overcoming some very real fears.

QUIETING THE VOICE

Sharing your journey is simple from a practical standpoint, but that doesn't make it easy. You may have concerns that stop you from experimenting with a more public approach to your work—a voice that tells you that you don't know enough, that people might judge you, or that learning in public could be a distraction, could damage your professional reputation, or could warp your priorities. Let's address these one by one.

"I DON'T KNOW ENOUGH."

Learning in public can feel daunting when comparing yourself to seasoned veterans who make it look easy and natural. It may also create the temptation to wait until you feel "ready" to get started. You don't need to be an expert to learn in public.

First, remember that "expertise" is a mirage; the closer you get, the more illusory it seems. That's why even old hands still get the jitters before putting themselves out there. Whatever your level of knowledge, learning in public will always be an act of vulnerability. In fact, this is the whole point: by sharing the journey instead of the result, you gain expertise over time without ever pretending to know everything about the topic.

In 2017, Danielle Simpson was teaching English online to Chinese children. She was working twelve-hour days, then spending two hours daily to write up feedback for parents—unpaid work that often boiled down to writing the same comments over and over again. Fed up with all the spreadsheets and documents, she finally asked her husband Arvid Kahl, a software developer, if they could build a simple software tool to automate some of the work. Kahl started building a prototype over the weekends. Two years later, they had grown the tool into a company that they sold for a life-changing amount of money.

Through this success, Kahl became convinced that not

every business needs venture capital to succeed. He had no formal expertise in what is known as bootstrapping, but he decided to study everything he could about the topic—and to share his learning along the way with other entrepreneurs. "Everybody has knowledge that they didn't have a couple of weeks ago or a couple of years ago," he told me. You're always a little ahead of someone else, which means sharing what you know could be helpful to at least one person. You might never get to know everything, but you'll always know enough to learn in public.

"PEOPLE MIGHT JUDGE ME."

There is something unnerving about having many eyes fixated on us, ready to judge our performance. This fear of public scrutiny can be found in many areas of our lives. Students may avoid speaking up in class. Others feel the pressure to nail first impressions in social situations. We conform to trends, scared of sticking out. Online, we avoid criticism by sharing only carefully curated personas.

Fear of public speaking is an acute symptom of how uncomfortable most of us are when we are standing in the public eye. It's one of the most common phobias—almost 30 percent of Americans say they fear speaking in front of a crowd. In fact, it's more commonly cited as a fear than death itself. Up until recently, I was one of those people who experienced intense anxiety around public speaking. In the lead-up to a big talk, I would have stomach cramps, difficulty concentrating, and insomnia at night. You can imagine how debilitating this all felt to me, as an educator who has to present quite often.

Learning in public shares many characteristics with public

speaking. How will people react? What will they say? Will I look stupid? From an evolutionary perspective, these questions make sense: for our ancestors, being evaluated favorably meant a higher chance of survival. So it's not so much that we fear being judged; we fear being judged *poorly*. Psychologists call this *fear of negative evaluation*, which we perceive as a genuine threat to our survival.

For many like me, this fear is not simply psychological, but physical as well. It activates the autonomic nervous system, which can lead to an increased heart rate, elevated blood pressure, and the infamous sweaty palms.

These physical reactions are rooted in a concrete fact: the more you share in public, the higher the likelihood you will eventually fail in public, whether it's a small mistake or a spectacular misstep. This can have consequences, from being called out for saying the wrong thing—as when public figures have to answer to statements they made years or even decades ago—to having your choices examined by both thoughtful critics and mean-spirited trolls.

Putting your work in progress out there feels dangerous when each idea risks critique, especially when you care about the work—then those critiques feel personal. So how do you contend with this fear?

A small personal experiment is a safe, low-stakes place to begin. By constantly showing up, the discomfort will progressively subside—the same principle of repeated exposure used by psychologists to help people reduce their anxiety in the presence of aversive stimuli.

This is how I managed to get a handle on my anxiety about public speaking. After reading many theoretical articles that did not help at all—I ended up with many strategies stored in my head, but still had those cramps in my stomach—

I signed up for a public speaking training course, which was focused on what sports coaches call "putting in the reps." All participants were required to give short talks without any preparation, again and again. The first time I went, my heart was pounding in my chest. The second time, it felt more like a manageable tightness. By the end of the training, I could remain calm and collected even when the assigned topic was "why rap music brings us together." Since then, I've made a pact to find at least one public speaking opportunity every quarter. I have presented in front of small groups as well as crowds of hundreds of people. I still have butterflies in my stomach before a talk, but no cramps.

And yet there was a very specific kind of public speaking that still paralyzed me: recording videos of myself. Speaking into a camera lens, we don't get any of the human signals we normally use to assess how we're coming across. We're also separated by time and space from the audience we're speaking to, which makes it hard to know how to connect. For these reasons, talking into a void creates an uncomfortable sense of dissociation and makes us hyperaware of ourselves, including our appearance and mannerisms.

You already know how I faced those fears: I designed a tiny experiment, which in this case lent itself perfectly to learning in public. I made a pact to film myself every day for ten days and to share it online. There were no rules or restrictions regarding the topic or format. My first video, where I made my public pledge, was very uncomfortable. My voice was shaky and I kept nervously squeezing my fingers. But people left encouraging comments and tips, and then the second one was easier. One day, at the airport just before boarding my flight, I even managed to record a video in a public place for the first time in my life.

I still felt self-conscious when the ten days were over, but I now was comfortable enough to hit *record* without any preparation. This experiment unlocked an entirely new mode of expression to add to my creative repertoire.

Just as with good old public speaking, "putting in the reps" is how we become comfortable with learning in public. The fear will never be completely gone, but it becomes more like a quiet companion than a cruel bully. You might even start to welcome the fear as a sign that you're about to do something you care about.

"IT MIGHT BE A DISTRACTION."

Will the time and effort required to document and share your work detract from your actual productivity? Will learning in public hinder your creative process? On first consideration, sharing your work in progress could become a distraction. Humans have limited attention spans, and the context switching between learning in public and doing the actual work could strain this capacity.

However, many public learners adeptly manage this balance. For instance, academics engage in public discourse while actively publishing research, maintaining visibility in their field while progressing in their projects. You might even set the scope of your pact so learning in public is inherently embedded into the experiment. When sharing is part of the project itself, you can learn in public without worrying about distraction.

Kristyn Sommer is a developmental psychologist who shares her works in progress via her social media channels. "It felt like a contribution I could make to the world," she told me. "It's about my life and experiences interspersed with science. It's about being autistic. It's about having two children. It's about healthcare accommodations for autistic people in the delivery room in hospitals."

Sommer doesn't consider her public platform a distraction from her scientific research. She agrees that the key is to integrate learning in public with the work you do already. "I'm already creating video lectures for my students, so I can do more videos for social media. I don't hold myself to a strict schedule. I just focus on sharing authentic content, building social support and connection."

Some of her colleagues told her she should focus on traditional academic measures of success, but Sommer disagrees. "They say to spend more time publishing papers, but I'm fairly certain that social media has gotten me a leg up in the academic world. It's made me stand out a bit more. I have just gotten a prestigious fellowship, and I have a feeling that part of the reason that was successful was because of my public platforms and the outreach work I do. Granting agencies see it as a form of dissemination." Learning in public has helped her shift from linear goals to a more generative way of ensuring her research has a wide impact and reaches the people who need it most.

Find opportunities to document and share that align with work you would be doing anyway. For instance, writers and artists share snippets of works in progress, giving fans a peek while maintaining momentum. Students document their learning publicly through "study grams" and project blogs. Leaders can share their ideation process, allowing stakeholders to engage early on. With this integrated approach, learning in public becomes part of your workflow. Rather than choosing between visibility and productivity, you can boost both simultaneously.

"IT MIGHT NEGATIVELY IMPACT MY PROFESSIONAL REPUTATION."

Sometimes following your curiosity can create certain tensions with your existing reputation. In many fields, reputation relies heavily on public perception, which can affect your career opportunities. How do you navigate the line between your authentic curiosity and your professional reputation?

Tracy Kim Townsend is an orthopedic surgeon who became interested in psychedelics as a tool for healing. "I was quite terrified about what my colleagues in conventional medicine would think of me," she told me. "I started opening up publicly about my interest in psychedelic medicines when I built my own professional website and started sharing on social media while I was still in residency. It was scary at first, but after several conversations with close friends in my community, I realized that I was in dire need of speaking my truth. My husband also really encouraged me to come out of the 'psychedelic closet' so that I could attract the kinds of collaborations that would help me shift onto that path."

Townsend eventually made the choice to leave her field and open her own practice. "Some people may think that it's crazy for me to be shifting gears like this, but I think it's even crazier to sit on the sidelines while the biggest paradigm shift in medicine is unfolding right before our eyes," she told me. Learning in public doesn't have to lead to a career change, but you won't know the full range of opportunities at your disposal until you start sharing your curiosity with the world. Ultimately, the key is to practice authenticity with boundaries, or what architects call an intimacy gradient between your emergent interests and your established reputation.

A simple way to safeguard your reputation is to start by

sharing with a small group of trusted people. Then you can share the highs and lows of your experiment without agonizing over every possible implication. If the results of your experiment make you reconsider some important career parameters or even lead to a change of career, then you can share your new professional project with a wider audience—when you're ready, and on your own terms.

"I MIGHT BECOME TOO FOCUSED ON EXTERNAL VALIDATION."

Sharing your work creates an audience effect, which is when the knowledge that others are observing you leads you to alter your behavior. The human brain is wired to respond to social feedback, which affects our self-perception and behavior—a response that translates to our interactions on social media. When shared publicly, your work becomes content for others to react to, distorting your priorities and skewing them toward pursuing public validation over personal values. Will you become too focused on external validation? How will you handle negative feedback or criticism?

Memoirists share intimate life details in service of a single story. But once the book is published, their identity continues to evolve. Like a rock star whose audience begs for their greatest hits, they are pressured to "be" their book in the world indefinitely. Author Stephanie Land faced intense scrutiny after publishing *Maid,* a raw memoir about her experiences as a single mom facing poverty and homelessness. After she sold the book and rights to a Netflix series, many assumed she had become rich and therefore removed from the problems she had written about, including a fan who was surprised to see her in first class, unaware the tickets were someone else's business expense.

Though her financial picture was still complicated, given the slow payouts of publishing, Land struggled with worries that she would be perceived as an impostor. Still, she tuned out the public noise and remained committed to saving consistently, focusing on what felt right for her and her family. This steady approach eventually allowed her to buy a house. "As a house cleaner, the thing that really got to me was the kids' bedrooms," she said. "I wanted that for my kids. Everything else is just a bonus."

Like Land, stay focused on your internal metrics of success. Don't let external expectations command your learning priorities. Instead, maintain a grounded practice aligned with your aspirations. Equally, be ready to listen when you receive constructive feedback. "There is no need to be afraid of starting a public platform as long as you show the world that you are ready to be proven wrong when presented with new evidence. Be ready to say: *I got it wrong, now we can learn together,*" says Kristyn Sommer.

It can help to limit time spent monitoring public feedback, or even to restrict who can comment on your posts on social media, so only people you follow can interact with your content. Not everyone's opinion about your learning journey is worth hearing.

AS ANAÏS NIN said, there will be a day when the risk to remain tight in a bud will feel more painful than the risk it takes to blossom. Then, despite any fears, you will know learning in public is worth it when you experience your first beautiful moment of connection that came from something you shared.

Start small and go (grow!) at your own pace. There is no

need to maintain a facade of expertise. Don't hide your uncertainty, your experiments, and your acts of becoming. Put them out there for others to learn from and weigh in on. Instead of flexing your expertise, flex your curiosity.

And if you find yourself in need of a final dose of courage, consider the perspective someone once shared with me moments before I stepped onstage: in a hundred years, you'll be dead, and so will every single person in the audience. So quit worrying and get out there.

12

✎ *Life Beyond Legacy*

Did you know that Giorgio Armani started a career in medicine before becoming one of the world's top fashion designers? That Harrison Ford was a carpenter for fifteen years before being catapulted to stardom with *Star Wars*? That Pope Francis II was a bouncer at a Buenos Aires nightclub before becoming the Pope?

As much as we love tales that reveal clear patterns amidst life's chaos, many success stories defy any legible narrative. They follow a nonlinear path, where curiosity and community, not continuity, determine each next step, and where each twist and turn provides unique insights that are later used to make a positive impact.

Ben Tossell is a shining example of how exploring one's curiosity and contributing to the growth of others can lead to a fulfilling life, even if it doesn't follow a conventional narrative. His early career saw him pitching a mobile app to pubs in London and failing to make a single sale, creating social media ads for an agency, and helping out at his dad's law firm. But around 2015, he found his way to a website called

Product Hunt, the online epicenter for tech tinkerers to share their projects.

Every day, dozens of products ranging from simple prototypes to full-fledged platforms were launched on Product Hunt in the hope of gaining their first users, while a vibrant community grew on the platform. Tossell was fascinated, and from his home in Cardiff in the United Kingdom, he decided to contribute by transcribing interviews of startup makers and publicizing members' projects. "I just wanted to talk about ideas and chat with people, to be helpful and connect with others who were building stuff." Soon Product Hunt hired him to engage with their European audience. Now an employee, Tossell did not let his creative spirit fade away. Instead, he experimented with side projects, including a chatbot and an AI art generator.

During this time, he started exploring the world of no-code tools, which allowed him to build digital products without extensive coding knowledge. Realizing how empowering these tools could be for others, Tossell created Makerpad, a platform dedicated to teaching people how to build digital products without code. By sharing his knowledge, Tossell aimed to empower a new generation of makers and entrepreneurs. Makerpad quickly took off, enabling thousands of individuals to bring their ideas to life. Tossell's approach, born out of his own curiosity and desire to help others, had a ripple effect that extended far beyond his personal journey, allowing him to raise funding to grow the platform even more. The impact of Makerpad did not go unnoticed. In 2021, Zapier, a startup worth $5 billion, acquired the platform.

With the launch of ChatGPT and the subsequent explosion of interest in AI, Tossell saw an opportunity to make a meaningful contribution in a new space. He started writing *Ben's Bites,* a newsletter about AI, to help others navigate this rapidly evolving landscape. "I wanted to surround myself in the AI world. How can I learn from everybody? How do I get in the room with these people? How can I play a small part here in doing something that could be helpful to people?" The answer was curating the space—scouring, decoding, and discussing the latest developments.

Again, his curiosity proved contagious. In its first year, his newsletter reached over one hundred thousand subscribers. And who knows where Tossell will go next? Even he doesn't know, and this is an essential part of the fun. What Tossell shares with many other curious minds profiled in this book is that he hasn't followed a predefined path for his career. Instead of focusing on a destination, he simply moves in the direction of his curiosity, constantly exploring where he can grow, who he wants to grow with, and how he can contribute positively to the world. This approach results in a fluid outlook on life, where progress is defined not only by what you learn and earn, but also by the positive impact you create.

When you leave behind the idea of a fixed vision for your career, you may end up on a path that looks quite wiggly. Each bend brings new experiences, lessons, and opportunities to connect with the world. Your curiosity and the people you meet along the way invite you to venture beyond your comfort zone. Your enduring willingness to adapt becomes yet another superpower in navigating the uncertainties of our world. Finally, by seeking out opportunities to contribute to the world around you, you derive immediate satisfaction and meaning even as the journey takes on a life of its own.

It's a rewarding way to approach your career, but there is

a challenge: How do you live by these principles in a world that values ready-made labels and neat, well-ordered résumés?

FROM LEGACY TO GENERATIVITY

Most of us want to live lives of meaning. But all too often, we search for that meaning in our professional seniority, promotions, academic achievements, or material possessions—and in the accolades and status that follow. These rewards are never enough. They keep us on a hedonic treadmill, always on a quest for the one accomplishment that will finally give us the feeling that we have at last secured our legacy.

The desire for legacy is the desire for evidence that your life, in the end, held meaning. Yet for someone on an unpredictable, nonlinear path, this kind of thinking can be self-defeating. After all, legacy is the most extreme kind of end game to set your sights on, since it happens *after your end*. And because legacy asks you to keep a scorecard of your successes, worrying about it can lead you to prioritize others' standards over your own. Legacy also steers us toward a view of impact that's based on scale: not what you built, but how big you built it.

To be successful at any age, on any path, and on your own terms, focus not on legacy but on *generativity*. Generativity is a psychological principle that emphasizes using your personal growth to positively impact the world around you. The term was coined by psychoanalyst Erik Erikson in the 1950s, who defined it as the "ability to transcend personal interests to provide care and concern for younger and older generations."

"The best long-term fuel source is some repeated act that energizes you in a way that then lets you become a generative person, who uses the energy to make things for others," wrote investor Patrick O'Shaughnessy. Instead of focusing on what you leave behind, generativity is about what you give now—actively contributing to your community, creating opportunities for others, and sharing your experiences in ways that enable collective growth.

Generativity isn't measured by scale but by the depth of connection in the here and now. It is built around the conversations you have, the positive impact of the work you produce, the lives you touch. Unlike legacy, which often fixates on leaving an outsized enduring mark, generativity is found in smaller everyday interactions and contributions—in the mentorship offered to a colleague, the knowledge shared in a community, or the support given to a local initiative. These actions, though they may seem modest, create a positive impact in real time, directly enriching lives.

This is how you discover your life's meaning—by focusing on your daily actions rather than the content of your future eulogy. When generativity becomes your focus, the immediate impact of your actions is all the motivation you need. Every pact you make, every shift, every "What if?" becomes not just a step in your own journey, but a chance to inspire and elevate others. Your career is no longer a linear ladder you climb alone, but a nonlinear path of shared discovery.

In the words of Irish poet David Whyte: "Perhaps the greatest legacy we can leave from our work is not to instill ambition in others, . . . but the passing on of a sense of sheer privilege, of having found a road, a way to follow, and then having been allowed to walk it, often with others, with all its difficulties and minor triumphs; the underlying primary gift, of having been a full participant in the conversation."

Again, deep down, our desire to have an impact on the world is a desire to be able to say: "I was here." But you are here right now. To live a good life, contribute good ideas, and nurture good relationships—that's ambitious, too. By adopting a few simple practices, you can transform the twists and turns into generative adventures, enabling you to grow with others—right here, right now.

KEYS FOR GENERATIVE ADVENTURES

When you optimize your life for generativity, you recognize that every bend in your professional life will not only equip you with new skills, knowledge, and relationships but also give you unique opportunities to contribute to the growth and development of others. Your nonlinear path allows you to create value in ways that may not be immediately apparent to others.

Yet, establishing credibility and communicating the impact of your contributions can be challenging without the traditional markers of success. Fortunately, the boundless opportunities of a generative life can be unlocked with what I call the Five Keys.

KEY #1. DO THE WORK FIRST

In a linear career, there is a clear hierarchy: everyone behind you and everyone in front of you. To take on a new challenge, you need to demonstrate that you have the necessary expertise to be promoted to the next stage, and then wait for someone to give you permission to start the work. These conventions create artificial friction and can limit your ability to make a meaningful impact.

In contrast, a generative approach is about proactively creating value. Instead of waiting for permission or validation, you can leverage your current resources and skills to produce tangible assets that demonstrate your ability to make a difference. That's exactly how Tossell approached all his projects: "I was doing proof of work because I didn't have any clout in the startup ecosystem. By doing so, I increased my surface area of luck. That's how I've ended up where I am."

Much like how skilled athletes strategically position themselves on the field, anticipate the game's direction, and leverage their team's strengths to make game-changing plays, increasing your surface area of luck involves choosing environments ripe with opportunity and connecting with a network of people who share your commitment to making a positive impact. "Luck isn't an independent variable but increases super-linearly with more surface area—you meet more people, make more connections between new ideas, learn patterns," said entrepreneur and investor Sam Altman.

And producing proof of work is one of the most effective ways to increase your surface area of luck. It gets you into new, ever more interesting rooms faster than any résumé. You not only demonstrate your problem-solving abilities but also showcase your knowledge in a tangible way. "No matter how isolated you are and how lonely you feel, if you do your work truly and conscientiously, unknown friends will come and seek you," wrote Carl Jung. Consistently producing relevant work builds trust within your professional community, which in turn increases your chances of being noticed by potential employers, investors, and collaborators, unlocking new career opportunities. This credibility not only opens up new career opportunities but also enables you to have a greater positive impact by attracting like-minded collaborators.

Instead of waiting for someone to sign off on your competence, build your experience by turning your interests into action, focusing on how you can create value for others. Designer Jack Butcher calls this a "permissionless apprenticeship," Seth Godin talks of the practice of "shipping" work, Cal Newport refers to the "craftsman mindset"—whatever you decide to call it, don't wait for approval; *do the work first.*

If you're interested in event planning, organize an event. If you want to explore a career as a software engineer, build an app and publish the code. For those aspiring to be chefs, create unique recipes and post them on social media. Want to be a fitness trainer? Film a series of workout videos and share it online. For interior design, redesign a room and create a visual blog about the process. Any of these could be supported by a pact.

Share your proof of work, and gradually build a reputation as someone who consistently creates value for others. Play and experiment without worrying about artificial milestones, focusing instead on how your work can contribute to the development of your community. Even if your path doesn't follow a neat line, the validation from your peers will come naturally when you continuously experiment and put your work out there in ways that positively impact those around you.

KEY #2. GROW LATERAL ROOTS

In the plant world, lateral roots play a crucial role in anchoring the plant securely into the soil, increasing water uptake, and facilitating the extraction of nutrients required for growth and development. These roots increase the territory of the root system, enabling the plant to access a wider range of resources.

We often talk of *upskilling,* but a generative approach allows you to expand your skills laterally. "By bringing more of experience under our current range of meaning and extending our range to embrace more things in more complex and abstract or sometimes ambiguous ways, we in effect enable ourselves to experience more of life in a given present, a given now," explained sociologist Andrew Abbott. Just as lateral roots are essential for a plant's growth and resilience, branching out beyond your primary area of expertise can help you thrive in today's rapidly evolving world. While others remain siloed in their field of expertise by stacking their skills vertically, your interdisciplinary experience will enable you to stand out and contribute to diverse fields in unique ways.

Take on a side project outside of what investors Warren Buffett and Charlie Munger call your core circle of competence—the kinds of projects that align with your interests even if they don't directly relate to your day job. These projects can help you develop new skills that enable you to contribute to diverse fields and create value for others. For instance, Matic Jurglič, a software developer, has taught himself how to 3D print incredibly lifelike concrete sculptures. Through his thriving Etsy store, he sells mini replicas of famous monuments and busts of influential people such as Nikola Tesla, Frida Kahlo, or Epictetus, and helps make art and history more accessible to a wider audience.

Like Jurglič, use online learning to pick up any necessary new skills outside your current field of expertise. Look for conferences on topics you know little about as an opportunity to gain exposure to new ideas while meeting new people. Seek out unlikely mentors who can provide guidance as your interests evolve. As you expand your knowledge and network, keep an eye out for unique opportunities to apply your skills in ways that benefit others and address unmet needs.

You can leverage your lateral skills to create value and positively impact others whether you're self-employed or working within an organization. Margaux Varipatis, a VP of business development at Universal Music, initially handed in her notice to pursue coaching but was offered a hybrid model by her employer. This arrangement allows her to provide coaching sessions to her colleagues for half a day every week, contributing to their personal and professional growth while still maintaining the security of her day job. "I thought, *Surely there's no way I can explore coaching while keeping my day job?*" she explained. "It's unfortunate that we rarely have those conversations because we don't think this model is available to us."

Cultivating lateral skills is a powerful way to live a generative life, enabling you to make an impact regardless of your employment status. By expanding your knowledge across disciplines and cultivating connections with diverse thinkers, you'll be able to approach challenges in innovative ways and contribute to solving complex problems that require an interdisciplinary perspective. Over time, you will create a distinctive atlas of skills that equip you to spot unique opportunities to positively impact the lives of others.

KEY #3. PRIORITIZE IMPACT OVER IMAGE

"When I quit *The New York Times* to be a full-time mother, the voices of the world said that I was nuts. When I quit it again to be a full-time novelist, they said I was nuts again," said author Anna Quindlen. "But I am not nuts. I am happy. I am successful on my own terms. Because if your success is not on your own terms, if it looks good to the world but does not feel good in your heart, it is not success at all."

While a clear personal brand may seem impressive in the short term, it can ultimately limit your potential to create value in the here and now. Success comes from following a path that allows you to positively impact the world around you, even if it doesn't conform to society's expectations. As former magazine editor Farrah Storr puts it, "You're not a commodity. You're a constantly shifting human being with a complex range of emotions, needs, and interests." Embracing this fluidity allows you to adapt and align your impact with your authentic ambitions.

Throughout history, many individuals have made significant contributions to society by refusing to be defined by a single role. Hedy Lamarr, known primarily as a film actress, allowed herself to explore her interest in technology and co-invented an early version of frequency-hopping spread spectrum, a foundation for modern wireless communication. Vera Wang's transition in her forties from figure skater and journalist to fashion designer allowed her to bring a unique perspective to the industry and inspire others to pursue their dreams at any age. Tim Ferriss, who began his career in data storage, has used his diverse experiences in entrepreneurship, writing, and investing to share valuable insights and tools for personal growth with millions of readers through his blog, podcast, and *4-Hour* book series.

When you allow your career to evolve with your curiosity, you open yourself up to new ways of creating value for others. A finance professional may develop innovative solutions that make financial services more accessible to under-served communities. A librarian could use podcasting to share knowledge and inspire others to explore new ideas. By offering corporate wellness training, a human resources professional could help employees lead healthier, more fulfilling lives both in and out of the office. And a mechanic with an interest in art may create metal sculptures that bring joy and beauty to others.

The rise of multipotentialites, slashies, and neo-generalists building portfolio careers reflects a growing recognition that our contributions need not be limited to a single field. Multi-hyphenate professionals—people who engage in such a wide range of occupations that they need multiple hyphens to describe their work—were once mostly found in the enter-tainment industry, where you would often meet an actor-singer-songwriter, but they are now common across many fields. By combining their diverse talents and interests, multi-hyphenates are finding new ways to create value and address complex challenges that require interdisciplinary solutions. Career chameleonization is not merely about personal fulfill-ment; it represents a shift toward a more generative approach to work, where the focus is on leveraging one's unique com-bination of skills and experiences to help others and drive meaningful change.

KEY #4. CLOSE THE LOOP TO OPEN DOORS

A path that zigzags across generative experiments can be per-ceived as confusing from the outside. However, many innova-tive thinkers and doers have woven together nonlinear careers by consistently closing the loop on each experiment and sharing their hard-won insights. By doing so, they transform each experiment into another thread building up to a canvas of expertise rooted in real-life experience, which they can then use to create value for others.

When you consistently finish what you start and reflect on the lessons learned, even if the outcome wasn't what you expected, people see you as someone who takes initiative, follows through, and gleans insights from every experience. Closing the loop demonstrates dependability and accountability, as well as your ability to help others navigate similar challenges—traits that build trust and open doors to new opportunities. This reputation can lead to more like-minded people seeking you out as a potential collaborator.

Serial entrepreneurs embody this principle. They often share detailed "postmortems" of their failed ventures, transparently analyzing what went wrong and what they learned. By doing so, they not only maintain the trust of their investors and team members but also contribute to the entrepreneurial community's collective wisdom, helping others avoid similar pitfalls and build on their insights. Even failure becomes generative.

When Evan Baehr's startup Outbox folded, he wrote a thoughtful postmortem analyzing why the business model was untenable. This commitment to closing the loop by transparently sharing key learnings enabled him to maintain the trust of investors and to take the company's team and what was left of their funding to spin it into an entirely new venture, Able Lending. Today, Baehr has become the embodiment of a generative life. He is a managing partner at a venture capital fund focused on human flourishing, wrote a book, teaches at the University of Texas, and hosts an educational podcast. By consistently reflecting and starting his next growth loop equipped with the collective lessons of the past, Baehr has transformed setbacks into springboards.

Closing the loop can be as simple as hosting a debrief meeting or writing an internal memo at work—where you can again use the Plus Minus Next template, explain what went well, what could have been handled better, and what you will focus on next. For bigger projects, you could consider writing a case study including interviews with key stakeholders. Sending a few thank-you notes is also a great way to close the loop. Whatever format you choose, the aim is to bring your experiment to a clear and deliberate conclusion, distill the lessons learned, and share them in a way that benefits others.

Consistently closing the loop builds trust in you as a person who will bring a commitment to learning and growth to any collaborative effort, especially those with unique challenges and unclear outcomes. Although your path won't feature the traditional milestones expected in a linear career, people will know they can count on you to get started, learn as you go, and share your insights in a way that contributes to the collective good—even if you fail, and perhaps especially so.

KEY #5. PLAY ALONG THE WAY

A generative approach to work recognizes the importance of playfulness alongside professionalism. Playfulness fosters creativity, exploration, and innovation. Finding joy in the present act of doing work can lead to discoveries that positively impact our career, others, and the world around us in ways we may not have initially imagined.

As Rory Sutherland, the vice-chair of Ogilvy UK and the cofounder of its Behavioural Science Practice, puts it: "It is much easier to be fired for being illogical than it is for being unimaginative. The fatal issue is that logic always gets you to exactly the same place as your competitors." What seems silly on the surface can lead to transformative results precisely because it operates free of constraints on seriousness. These unconventional approaches often result in solutions and ideas that address unmet needs and create value in unexpected ways.

Chelsey White's journey shows how playful generativity can lead to both personal fulfillment and value for others. White started baking cakes and filming them for fun. "I really just needed a creative outlet," she explained. As people started asking how they could order her cakes, she realized that her personal creative outlet could be transformed into a way to create delight for others. About a year into selling her cakes, she started making a decent profit. After four years, she made the switch to baking cakes full time. Yet to this day, her focus is on having fun. "If you don't enjoy it and are just trying to make money, I think you're not going to be successful," she said.

Framing experiments as "just for fun" alleviates the pressure of meeting certain expectations, both self-imposed and from others, which can lead to creating value in unexpected ways. Take the case of entrepreneur Josh Pigford, who has launched dozens of ventures, including an action figures store, a quiz builder, a package tracking app, an online community for pug owners, a wealth management tool, a music industry simulation game, and handmade homewares. How does he decide what experiments to keep working on? "I'll choose to shut something down if I'm not having fun anymore," he told me. While not all of Pigford's ventures were exponentially successful, many of them have positively impacted the lives of their customers by addressing unique needs or providing entertaining experiences. One example is the small but profitable business that emerged from his experiment with laser-engraving tweets into wood.

Injecting playfulness into your work can liberate you to test ideas where you have limited knowledge—the exact kinds of ideas that could have an important impact not only on your career but also on the lives of others. By exploring unobvious paths and reframing problems in entertaining and intellectually stimulating ways, you open up new possibilities for creating value and making a positive difference in the world.

ULTIMATELY, THE MOST powerful tool at your disposal is your ability to reinvent, reimagine, and reshape your career journey in ways that generate value for yourself and others, as the world around you itself transforms.

MADE FOR YOUR SEARCHING

Think back on your previous career decisions and projects you have worked on. Be honest with yourself: Could you have predicted which ones went well, which ones failed, which ones opened new doors, which ones were fun, which ones were a pain?

If you manage to free yourself from the hindsight bias, you will realize that you had no idea where each choice would take you and what the journey would feel like. Some of what seem like our most benign decisions can lead to surprising results; some of our most exciting projects can fizzle out.

This unpredictability is not a bug but a feature of a generative approach to life. By embracing the unknown and staying open to serendipity, you create space for unexpected opportunities to emerge—opportunities to learn, grow, and create value in ways you may not have initially imagined.

Focus on the present moment and ask yourself: *How can I use my skills and experiences to positively impact the people around me right now?*

You are an evolving canvas, an unfolding story, a great work in the making. All you can do is imagine a world of possibilities and keep on experimenting until you discover what works. Each experience, whether a success or a failure by conventional standards, opens new doors, which you'll pass through with new capability and wisdom. "What an adventure!" is what you want to exclaim in a few years when you look back on your path and see all the wiggles and question marks characteristic of an experimental approach to life.

Ultimately, living a generative life is about embracing the adventure of not knowing where your path will lead while trusting that you will find fulfillment along the way. John Keats famously wrote that though life is fleeting and sometimes filled with darkness, the beauty to be found offers a perpetual source of wonder to those who seek it.

Your life is made for your searching—not for a predefined destination, but for the joy of discovery and the satisfaction of knowing that your efforts are making a positive difference in the world. So go forth and explore with an open mind and a generous heart.

Hello, Experimental Life

When this book was just an outline, a live-action remake of *Pinocchio* came out, and I rediscovered my love for the classic story of a puppet who wished to come to life. As a kid, I was fascinated with the magic involved, and still today I relate to the yearning to explore, the itch to tell stories, and the playful embrace of curiosity that inevitably leads to mishaps, but ultimately helps you grow.

What makes *you* come alive? Ultimately, there is no more noble ambition than answering this question. Like Pinocchio, we all yearn to live life to its fullest. But as our paths likely won't involve fairy godmothers, the magic for us lies in discovering the experiences that light that spark.

Finding this magic isn't straightforward. It's a process of trial and error. It involves tinkering with your thoughts, challenging your beliefs, and stepping out of your comfort zones. And just as in scientific experiments, where a different input or environment can affect the outcome, the formula you once discovered may change as your circumstances, your perspectives, and even your tastes evolve.

I haven't figured it all out myself, and I know I never will. I'm just excited to share what I have learned so far, and I selfishly want more people on the journey with me so I can learn from them in return.

The following principles are a distillation of the most important ideas in this book so you can consult them whenever you need a refresher. Think of it as an experimentalist manifesto: an exhortation to live a life of systematic curiosity, where uncertainty is a feature and not a bug, where inner resistance is a welcome source of information, and where the generative now matters more than your legacy.

Forget the finish line. In our quest for personal and professional growth, we often constrain ourselves within the narrow pathways of linear goals. Instead of chasing the next milestone, embrace the liminal and open yourself to a world of possibilities beyond the outcomes you can imagine today.

Unlearn your scripts. Since childhood, internalized patterns form cognitive scripts that subtly guide our actions in relationships, work, and education. By unlearning these scripts, you can explore life's full spectrum of experiences, consider unobvious paths, and nurture your ever-changing curiosity rather than seeking one all-absorbing passion.

Turn doubts into experiments. Confidence is built through action. When in doubt, run a personal experiment using a pact—a time-bound commitment to a repeatable action that follows this format: **I will [action]**

for [duration]. You are now the scientist of your own life, with a mindset of openness and curiosity, allowing you to learn from each iteration even if you don't know the destination.

Let go of the chronometer. Shift your focus from Chronos, the quantitative definition of time, to Kairos, which emphasizes the unique quality of each moment. Manage your energy, executive function, and emotions rather than your minutes. Optimize for the depth of experience rather than the speed of achievement. Remember that life is not about how much we do, but how well we do.

Make friends with procrastination. Procrastination is not an enemy to be conquered, but a meaningful signal that something is amiss—a mismatch between your rational aspirations (head), your emotional needs (heart), and your practical skills (hand). Approach procrastination from a place of curiosity to identify its cause and adjust your course of action.

Embrace imperfection. You cannot excel at everything simultaneously. Long-term excellence comes not from maintaining perfect balance but from prioritizing what is most important at any given moment. Identify perfectionist patterns, challenge unrealistic targets, and aim for intentional imperfection. This is not a permanent compromise, but rather the chance to choose carefully which areas of your life or work you will temporarily allow to be less than perfect so that you can excel in others.

Design growth loops. If you want to grow, action is nothing without reflection. Master metacognition, the practice of reflecting on your thinking, so that you become not only aware of your thoughts and emotions but skilled at regulating them. By leveraging this mental awareness, you will live more intentionally, make smarter decisions, and evolve beyond automatic responses to the challenges you face.

Broaden the decision frame. There is more to success than scaling up. You have three choices: persist with your current path if it's rewarding, pause if it's proving unfulfilling, or pivot to better suit your evolving circumstances. Every crossroads offers a chance to learn and grow; spend time exploring all internal and external factors before choosing your path forward.

Dance with disruption. When life's song abruptly changes, relax and listen. Stay nimble. Explore your subjective experience with curiosity before confronting the objective consequences of the disruption. Then chaos can become a source of transformation.

Seek fellow explorers. The world is not just changing; it's becoming increasingly complex. Leverage the power of social flow by being an active participant in communities. Cultivate your existing relationships with intention. Share your skills and knowledge to foster collective curiosity. Connecting with others will not only expand your horizons and amplify your impact, but also provide a safety net, making you more resilient to change.

Learn in public. Resist the urge to work behind closed doors. Instead, learn in public—sharing not just your achievements, but also your false starts and mistakes. Put in the reps. Practice radical transparency so your growth aligns with your true aspirations. Celebrate the process as much as the success that follows.

Let go of your legacy. Instead of working hard toward a beautiful eulogy, focus on the generative present. Navigate life's winding paths with a sense of adventure: follow your curiosity and invest your energy not in what will be remembered about you, but in the tangible impact you can have right now.

I can't wait to hear about your first tiny experiment. Remember that you are the lead scientist of your life. There is no universal formula. You are unique and nothing about your future is fixed. Whether you are twenty or seventy, you can move in any direction your curiosity leads.

In the liminal space called life, we are in perpetual transition from one identity to another, from one question to the next, a succession of twists and turns, each an opportunity to learn about the world and connect with others. Success is the lifelong experiment of discovering what makes you feel most alive.

APPENDIX

Experimentalist Toolkit

This is a quick-access reference guide for approaching any challenge with curiosity and finding success without a road map. In true scientific fashion, ask yourself how each tool can apply to your life and feel free to tailor them to fit your specific situation.

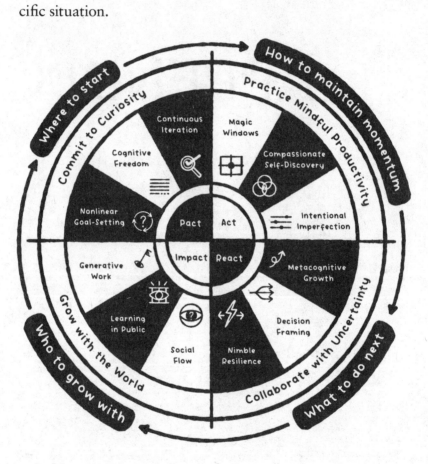

Just start by selecting the question that best describes your current situation and go to the corresponding quadrant in the toolkit.

- **Where** can I start?
- **How** can I maintain momentum?
- **What** can I do next?
- **Who** can I keep growing with?

Once you have identified your question, use the tools you discovered in this book to navigate the situation:

Pact: Commit to Curiosity

Adopt an experimental mindset with the Three Mental Shifts (p. 37).

Challenge cognitive scripts with Field Notes (p. 50).

Design small iterative experiments with a Pact (p. 57).

Act: Practice Mindful Productivity

Open magic windows with a Kairos Ritual (p. 92).

Listen to procrastination with the Triple Check (p. 106).

Leverage imperfection with the Ambition Dials (p. 124).

React: Collaborate with Uncertainty

Create metacognitive growth loops with Plus Minus Next (p. 135).

Broaden the decision frame with the Steering Sheet (p. 159).

Dance with disruption with the Two-Step Reset (p. 165).

Impact: Grow with the World

Unlock social flow with a Curiosity Circle (p. 186).

Learn in public with the Public Pillars (p. 197).

Do generative work with the Five Keys (p. 222).

You can download a printable version of this toolkit at https://nesslabs.com/toolkit.

Reflection Guide

The following prompts are simple tools for self-discovery. Answering each question will deepen your understanding of the themes discussed in each chapter of the book. You can reflect on these prompts at the end of the corresponding chapter or address them all at once as part of a more comprehensive reflection exercise.

1. Reflect on a time when setting a goal felt limiting rather than motivating. What benefits might have come from a more fluid, open-ended approach?
2. Think about the pressure to find a singular purpose in your professional or personal life. How has this affected your choices?
3. Recall a recent source of doubt or fear. How could you turn this into a small iterative experiment to learn and grow, rather than a barrier?
4. How do you currently manage your time? Reflect on how shifting from a focus on efficiency to a focus on the quality of your experiences might impact your daily life.
5. Consider a recent instance of procrastination. What might it have been signaling, and how could you address the underlying issue constructively?
6. Identify an area in your life where perfectionism holds you back. How could embracing intentional

imperfection help you move forward while still being satisfied with your work?

7. Reflect on a time when you learned from trial and error. How did this metacognitive process contribute to your growth, and how could you apply it more deliberately in the future?

8. Think about a significant decision you've made in the past. Did you choose to persist, pause, or pivot? What did you learn from the outcome?

9. Describe a disruption you recently faced. How did you react, and what steps could you take to better navigate and learn from such disruptions in the future?

10. Consider your communities and their alignment with your interests. To what degree are they supporting your growth—and if they're not, what steps can you take to change that?

11. Recall an example of when you learned something new in a public setting. How did this openness affect your learning process and the support you received?

12. Think about the impact you want to have right now, rather than your long-term legacy. What small, meaningful actions could you take today to contribute to your community in a generative way?

Whether you're journaling on your own, working with a coach, or participating in a book club discussion, use these twelve questions to explore your thoughts and challenge your assumptions, and develop an experimental mindset.

To make the most of the prompts, you might find these guidelines helpful:

- **Take your time:** Allow yourself the space to give each question careful thought. There are no right or wrong answers—only your personal experience.

- **Be honest:** Only genuine self-reflection can unlock actionable insights. Express what truly comes to mind, even if it's unexpected or feels uncomfortable.

- **Reflect regularly:** Consistent reflection can help you understand and observe your growth over time. Consider adding these prompts to your regular metacognitive practice.

- **Discuss openly:** If you're in a book club or coaching setting, share your reflections with others. Radical transparency can enrich your perspective and strengthen the connection with your peers.

BONUS RESOURCE

The Art of Mind Gardening

In true experimental fashion, this book has gone through many iterations. The title changed three times and the outline a dozen times. As for the content itself? I've lost count.

As I was writing, one chapter took on a life of its own. It kept growing and exploring ideas that went beyond the scope of this book. I wanted to dive deeper into applying an experimental mindset to knowledge management, but my editor and I realized that cramming everything into one chapter wouldn't do it justice.

We knew it deserved its own dedicated space, so we decided to make it a stand-alone resource. This way, you can explore these ideas at your own pace, without interrupting the flow of the book.

You can download it here: https://nesslabs.com/mgbonus.

ADAPTABILITY: The ability to adjust to new conditions and modify strategies accordingly.

ALIGNED ALIVENESS: A harmonious state where one's thoughts, emotions, and actions are in alignment, making tasks feel appropriate, exciting, and doable.

ANALYSIS PARALYSIS: Overthinking a situation to the point that a decision or action is never taken.

CAREER LADDER: The traditional linear progression of career advancement within an organization or field, often contrasted with nonlinear portfolio careers.

COGNITIVE SCRIPTS: Subconscious mental frameworks that guide individuals' perceptions and actions based on past experiences and societal norms.

COLLECTIVE INTELLIGENCE: The group intelligence that emerges from the collaboration of many individuals, enhancing problem-solving and innovation.

COMMITMENT DEVICE: A method used to bind oneself to a plan of action that might otherwise be difficult to accomplish.

COMMUNITY ARCHITECT: Individual who shapes and builds communities, fostering generative environments for meaningful connection, shared learning, and collective growth.

CONE OF UNCERTAINTY: A visual mental model that illustrates the increasing range of possible outcomes over time, reflecting the inherent uncertainty in predicting future events.

CONSEQUENCE CASCADE: The series of outcomes that result from a single action or decision.

CREATIVE CONSTRAINTS: Limitations or challenges that fuel innovation and problem-solving.

CROWDPLEASER SCRIPT: A cognitive script that guides actions based on the desire to please or gain approval from others.

CURIOSITY CIRCLE: A community centered around genuine connection and peer learning, where participation is based on curiosity rather than expertise.

DECISION FRAME: The context and perspective through which choices are evaluated and made, including the assumptions, objectives, and boundaries that shape decision-making processes.

DISRUPTION: Significant change or interruption that challenges the status quo.

EMOTIONAL AGILITY: The ability to fluidly adapt and respond to emotional experiences, enhancing overall well-being and performance.

EPIC SCRIPT: A cognitive script that drives actions based on the pursuit of grand or heroic achievements.

EUSTRESS: Positive stress that motivates and enhances performance, as opposed to distress, which is negative and paralyzing.

EXECUTIVE FUNCTION: Cognitive processes that enable planning, focusing attention, remembering instructions, and managing multiple tasks successfully.

EXPERIMENTAL MINDSET: An attitude of openness and curiosity, focused on learning from each experience rather than achieving a specific outcome.

FLOW STATE: A mental state of deep immersion and engagement in an activity, often leading to high levels of creativity and productivity.

FREE-FLOATING ANXIETY: Persistent worry that is not tied to any specific threat or situation.

GENERATIVITY: Using personal growth to positively impact the world, focusing on meaningful contributions in the present rather than long-term legacy.

GOOD MISTAKES: Errors or undesired outcomes that prompt reflection, leading to growth and learning.

GROWTH LOOPS: Cycles of trial, error, and learning that contribute to continuous improvement and development.

INTENTIONAL IMPERFECTION: Deliberately choosing to be temporarily mediocre in some areas of life and work to excel in others, thus prioritizing long-term excellence over short-term perfection.

ITERATIVE PROCESS: A method involving repeated cycles of testing, feedback, and refinement.

KAIROS RITUAL: Small, repeatable action designed to quickly shift one's mood, reconnect to the body, or provide a chance to check in with oneself.

LATERAL SKILLS: Diverse skills acquired across different fields, enabling innovative problem-solving and interdisciplinary contributions.

LEARNING IN PUBLIC: The process of acquiring knowledge and skills in a community or open setting, sharing progress, mistakes, and lessons learned.

LIMINALITY: The transitional phase between two stages or conditions, often characterized by ambiguity and uncertainty.

LINEAR GOALS: Goals that follow a predetermined, step-by-step path toward a specific end.

MAGIC WINDOWS: Periods of peak creativity and productivity that occur when fully immersed in an activity that captures complete attention.

MAXIMALIST BRAIN: The tendency to want to always go with the bigger option or engage in too many activities simultaneously, leading to difficulty in prioritizing and completing tasks.

METACOGNITION: Curiosity directed at one's inner world—thoughts, emotions, and beliefs—to gain greater insights and improve decision-making and emotional regulation.

MINDFUL PRODUCTIVITY: The practice of being present and fully engaged in the task at hand, rather than merely focusing on efficiency.

MULTIPOTENTIALITE: An individual with diverse interests and creative pursuits, often excelling in multiple fields.

NONLINEAR PATH: A journey that does not follow a straight, predictable trajectory, but involves unexpected changes, detours, and experiences.

OPEN SCIENCE: The practice of openly documenting the research process, including missteps and exploratory paths, to invite collaboration and accelerate discovery.

PACT: A pledge to engage in a particular activity for a predetermined period, driven by curiosity rather than outcome.

PERCEPTION-ACTION CYCLE: The ongoing interaction between the brain's perception of the environment and subsequent actions, guiding decisions based on continuous and often subconscious feedback.

PERSONAL EXPERIMENT: A self-designed, time-bound commitment to a repeatable action based on a pact aimed at learning and growth.

PLANNING FALLACY: The tendency to underestimate the time, costs, and risks of future actions while overestimating the benefits, often leading to overly optimistic plans.

PLUS MINUS NEXT: A metacognitive tool to celebrate accomplishments, evaluate outcomes, and adapt decisions, fostering continuous improvement.

POOLING EFFECT: The benefit of accessing a community's collective knowledge, skills, and resources, enabling meaningful progress beyond an individual's capacity.

PORTFOLIO CAREER: A career path that involves multiple roles or projects simultaneously, rather than a single long-term job.

PROCRASTINATION: The act of delaying or postponing tasks, which can signal underlying needs or conflicts.

PROOF OF WORK: Demonstrating abilities through tangible outputs rather than relying on titles or credentials.

PROVENANCE: The context and history associated with a work of art, including its creation and ownership.

QUALITY OF EXPERIENCE: The subjective value and satisfaction derived from how time is spent, rather than the quantity of tasks completed.

RADICAL TRANSPARENCY: The practice of openly sharing processes, decisions, and mistakes to invite collaboration and build trust.

RESILIENCE: The capacity to recover quickly from difficulties and adapt to change.

RESPONSE 1: An automatic reaction characterized by discomfort, fear, and anxiety in the face of uncertainty, triggering a fight/flight/freeze response.

RESPONSE 2: An autonomous reaction characterized by delight, calm, and curiosity in the face of uncertainty, triggering an engage/explore/experiment response.

RIPPLE EFFECT: The impact that one action or event can have on a larger system, spreading and influencing other areas beyond the initial focus.

SAFETY EFFECT: The emotional and practical support provided by a community, enhancing individual resilience and stability.

SALON: A gathering where like-minded individuals exchange ideas, often leading to significant creative and intellectual growth.

SELF-ANTHROPOLOGY: The practice of observing and analyzing one's own behaviors, habits, and patterns to gain insights and design better experiments.

SELF-COMPLEXITY: The degree to which an individual's sense of identity is differentiated and compartmentalized, influencing resilience and emotional stability.

SELF-CONSISTENCY FALLACY: The mistaken belief that one must always act consistently with past behaviors or decisions, potentially limiting growth and adaptability.

SEQUEL SCRIPT: A cognitive script that limits future actions based on past events and outcomes.

SEQUENTIAL FOCUS: The practice of concentrating on one task at a time, moving on to the next task only after the first one is completed.

SOCIAL FLOW: The enhanced collective experience and mindful productivity achieved through group collaboration.

STEERING SHEET: A framework for making decisions by broadening the decision frame and considering both internal and external factors.

SUNK COST FALLACY: The cognitive bias that leads one to continue a commitment based on previously invested resources (time, money, effort) even when it would be more rational to abandon it.

SYSTEMATIC CURIOSITY: Living a life of curiosity where external uncertainty is embraced and inner resistance is viewed as a useful source of information.

TOXIC PRODUCTIVITY: An obsession with efficiency that leads to burnout, stress, and a neglect of well-being and personal fulfillment.

TRANSACTIVE MEMORY: A shared system for encoding, storing, and retrieving information within a group, where individuals rely on one another for different areas of expertise.

TRIPLE CHECK: A tool for listening to procrastination signals by considering rational (head), emotional (heart), and practical (hand) factors.

TYRANNY OF PURPOSE: The pressure to find a single overarching purpose in life or career.

UNDERLYING NEEDS: Fundamental psychological or emotional drives that influence behavior and decision-making.

ACKNOWLEDGMENTS

This book may be titled *Tiny Experiments*, but it has been the most significant and transformative experiment of my life. As I sit down to write these acknowledgments, I'm struck by the sheer number of brilliant minds who made this book possible. From the first spark of inspiration to the final pages, I have been fortunate to be surrounded by a community that challenged me, supported me, and helped me navigate these new territories. To everyone who contributed to this book in any way, please know that you have left a lasting impact on my life. Without you, this book would not exist.

My deepest gratitude goes to Megan Newman and the incredible team at Avery/Penguin Random House for believing in a first-time author. I am indebted to my editor, Jacob Surpin, whose careful reading and insightful suggestions have elevated the quality of this work. A special thank-you to Sara Grace for being an extraordinary thought partner and helping me articulate my ideas clearly. I am also profoundly grateful to my agent, Lisa DiMona, for her unwavering support and guidance as I discovered the ins and outs of the publishing world.

I am grateful to Tiago Forte, who not only encouraged me to embark on this journey but also generously shared his experiences and lessons learned. To James Clear, thank you for convincing me to write this book in English, even though it's not my native language. You gave me the confidence to hold out for the perfect English-language publisher. I am also indebted to my amazing network of internet friends and fellow writers for their support and feedback. Ali Abdaal, Alyssa X, Amanda Natividad, Ana Lorena Fábrega, Ankit Shah, Arvid Kahl, Ben Meer, Ben Mercer, Charlotte Crowther, Dan Shipper, David Hoang, Duke Stump, Gemma Milner, Izzy Sealey, Jay Clouse, Jenny Wood, Jo Franco, Jonny Miller, Khe Hy, Lawrence Yeo, Marie Poulin, Nat Eliason, Nick Gray, Nick Milo, Nir Eyal, Noah Kagan, Oliver Sauter, Paul Millerd, Polina Pompliano, Rand Fishkin, Ryder Carroll, Sarah Stockdale, Simone Stolzoff, Steph Smith, Ryan Mayer, and Yina Huang—whether it was through long heart-to-heart conversations, quick voice notes filled with advice, or introductions that helped move the project forward, each of you played an integral role in bringing this book to life.

The Ness Labs community has been an endless source of inspiration and motivation throughout this journey. The thought-provoking conversations and stories of how these ideas have influenced your lives have kept me going. I am particularly thankful to community members who volunteered as beta readers—Bronagh Mallon, Ida Josefiina, Madi Taskett, Monica Lim, Nivi Achanta, Olivia Patterson, Oran Kangas, Sarah Toner, Susan Tian, and Visakan Veerasamy— for taking the time to read early versions of this work and offering detailed feedback that helped shape this book into what it is today. To all the generous interviewees who took the time to answer my questions candidly, openly, and vulnerably—thank you. Your input has been invaluable to this book, and I hope I have done justice to your experiences in these pages.

To my team at Ness Labs—Maame Yaa Serwaa Bona-Mensa, Farah Guzman, Haikal Kushahrin, and Joseph Opoku—I am grateful for your exceptional work and dedication in helping me grow and support the Ness Labs community. Thank you as well to Stephanie Lee and Steven Alexander Young for your strategic guidance in helping this book reach those who need it most.

I want to express my special thanks to my PhD supervisors, Professor Eleanor Dommett and Dr. Vincent Giampietro, for supporting my hypercurious mind and giving me the flexibility to explore my many interests. Your trust made it possible for me to write this book while pursuing my doctoral studies at King's College London. I'm excited to keep on conducting research together in the years to come.

Many thanks to the mentors who shaped my professional journey at Google and beyond: Lorraine Twohill, Amy Brown, Nishma Patel Robb, Feng Xu, Matt Waddell, Torsten Schuppe, James Elias, Yonca Dervisoglu, Steve Vranakis, and Peter Vesterbacka, as well as the (A)PMMs I had the privilege of starting my career with.

To my friends—Charis, Anaïs, Cannelle, Corin, Tobi, Paco, Inès, Jem, Brian, Luke, Sam, Ed, Paraskevi, Seetha, Valou, Hugo, Lilou, Matt, Lucho, Elyass, Loulou, Niko, Niri, Thomas, Agathe, Gastón, Krzysztof, Pedro, Juliette, Grace, Ann, and Henri—thank you for being there for me through delight and doubt alike. Your friendship means the world to me. Special thanks to my furry friend, Mister Squirrel, who always knows when to tap on the window with his little paws, reminding me to take breaks and share some almonds. His impromptu visits provided much-needed moments of delight during long writing days.

I am eternally thankful to my parents, Sandra and Serge, who have always made me feel like anything is possible. Thank you for embracing growth and change alongside me, showing me that we never stop evolving. Here's to more travels, tattoos, and transformation together. To my siblings, Morgane, Xavier, and Samir, with whom I've shared silly and serious moments, secrets, and adventures—seeing the incredible people you've become fills me with joy.

To my partner, Paul, who gives me the absolute freedom to explore and grow—thank you for your unshakable belief in me and your unconditional love. I am excited to continue this journey of discovery with you by my side in all the in-betweens of this experimental life.

Finally, I dedicate this book to my grandmother, Oma, who never had the opportunity to learn to read or write and would be so proud.

NOTES

INTRODUCTION: GOODBYE, LINEAR LIFE

13. **known in ancient times as "the city of magic":** Before being renamed after an Arab general, Sidi Okba was called Madinat as-Sihr, which means "city of magic." See Abd Allâh ibn ʿAbd al-ʿAzīz Abū ʿUbayd al-Bakrī, *Description de l'Afrique septentrionale,* trans. Mac Guckin de Slane (Paris: Imprimerie Impériale de Paris, 1859).

14. **the fortified French city of Dinan:** R. E. Durand, E. Launay, and H. Legénisel, "Histoire de Dinan à travers les âges avec plan actuel," *Annales de Bretagne et des Pays de l'Ouest* 36, no. 1 (1924): 127–30.

14. **one of the largest medievalist events in Europe:** This is the Fête des Remparts (Ramparts Festival), with jousting tournaments, balls, a parade, and a big medieval market, which has taken over the town of Dinan every other year since 1983.

16. **"a sort of petite existential shock therapy":** Irvin D. Yalom, *Staring at the Sun: Overcoming the Terror of Death* (Hoboken, NJ: Jossey-Bass, 2008), 99–100.

17. **"the healthcare startups you need to know about":** Matt Reynolds, "These Are the Healthcare Startups You Need to Know About," *WIRED,* March 16, 2018, https://www.wired.com/story/best-health care-startups-wired-health-2018.

18. **a prestigious startup accelerator:** This accelerator is called Entrepreneur First. I made many friends there, so I jokingly call it "the friendship accelerator."

18. **from one kind of hyperfocused outcome-driven pursuit to another:** Paul Millerd calls this the "last stand," when we double down on our old ways despite this path clearly being wrong. His book *The Pathless Path* narrates how he finally broke free and designed a life of fluid exploration.

18. **the Hero's Journey:** Joseph Campbell, *The Hero with a Thousand Faces* (Princeton: Princeton University Press, 1968), 30.

20. **I called it Ness Labs:** In true tinkerer fashion, I experimented with a few names. Early readers of the newsletter would have known it as *The Creative Nomad* and later *Maker Mind*, until I settled on *Ness Labs*.

21. **enrich your life with systematic curiosity:** A. L. Le Cunff, "Systematic Curiosity as an Integrative Tool for Human Flourishing: A Conceptual Review and Framework," *Integrative Psychological and Behavioral Science* (2024): 1–19.

CHAPTER 1: WHY GOAL SETTING IS BROKEN

26. **her first book:** Amelia Earhart, *20 Hrs., 40 Min.: Our Flight in the Friendship* (New York: G. P. Putnam's Sons, 1928).

27. **"liking to experiment" as a common thread:** Amelia Earhart, *The Fun of It: Random Records of My Own Flying and of Women in Aviation* (New York: Brewer, Warren & Putnam, 1932).

27. **learn first and foremost through movement:** David L. Gallahue and John C. Ozmun, *Understanding Motor Development: Infants, Children, Adolescents, Adults* (Boston: McGraw Hill, 2006).

27. **children ask more than a hundred questions:** Michael M. Chouinard, "Children's Questions: A Mechanism for Cognitive Development," *Monographs of the Society for Research in Child Development* 72, no. 1 (2007): vii–ix, 1–112.

28. **focusing on self-packaging:** Daniel J. Lair, Katie Sullivan, and George Cheney, "Marketization and the Recasting of the Professional Self: The Rhetoric and Ethics of Personal Branding," *Management Communication Quarterly* 18, no. 3 (2005): 307–43.

28. **"First say to yourself what you would be":** From Epictetus, *The Works of Epictetus: His Discourses, in Four Books, the Enchiridion, and Fragments*, trans. Thomas Wentworth Higginson (New York: Thomas Nelson and Sons, 1890).

29. **you may have heard of as SMART goals:** George T. Doran, "There's a S.M.A.R.T. Way to Write Management's Goals and Objectives," *Management Review* 70, no. 11 (1981): 35–36.

29. **feeling stuck when it comes to their next steps:** Researchers refer to frozen goals, which are goals that we continue to commit to but do not actively pursue for a variety of reasons.

29. **"No goals, just vibes":** Amil Niazi, "Losing My Ambition," *The Cut*, March 25, 2022, https://www.thecut.com/2022/03/post-pandemic-loss -of-ambition.html.

29. **the end of ambition:** Noreen Malone, "The Age of Anti-Ambition," *New York Times Magazine*, February 15, 2022, https://www.nytimes .com/2022/02/15/magazine/anti-ambition-age.html.

30. **orientational metaphors:** Ahmadova Ramila Isfandiyar Gizi, "Interpretation of Space Through Metaphors," *Advances in Social Sciences Research Journal 5*, no. 10 (2018).

30. **leads to analysis paralysis:** Ram Charan, "Conquering a Culture of Indecision," *Harvard Business Review 79*, no. 4 (2001): 74–82, 168.

30. **"merely justifications to keep themselves busy":** Christopher K. Hsee, Adelle X. Yang, and Liangyan Wang, "Idleness Aversion and the Need for Justifiable Busyness," *Psychological Science 21*, no. 7 (2010): 926–30.

31. **linear goals promote an individualistic mentality:** Terence R. Mitchell and William S. Silver, "Individual and Group Goals When Workers Are Interdependent: Effects on Task Strategies and Performance," *Journal of Applied Psychology 75*, no. 2 (1990), 185–93.

32. **the Red Queen effect:** Pamela J. Derfus et al., "The Red Queen Effect: Competitive Actions and Firm Performance," *Academy of Management Journal 51*, no. 1 (2008): 61–80.

32. **Alice says to the Queen:** Lewis Carroll, *Alice's Adventures in Wonderland & Through the Looking-Glass* (New York: Bantam Classics, 1984).

32. **French philosopher René Girard:** René Girard, "Présentation de la Théorie Mimétique," *Océaniques*, broadcast by Alain Joubert, Michel Cazenave, and Jean-Daniel Verhaeghe, March 10, 2014, Association Recherches Mimétiques, https://youtu.be/d9z0BmMCBC4.

34. **protect us from unknown risks:** Jack Grinband, Joy Hirsch, and Vincent P. Ferrera, "A Neural Representation of Categorization Uncertainty in the Human Brain," *Neuron 49*, no. 5 (2006): 757–63.

34. **problematic when a clear answer isn't readily available:** Dan W. Grupe and Jack B. Nitschke, "Uncertainty and Anticipation in Anxiety: An Integrated Neurobiological and Psychological Perspective," *Nature Reviews Neuroscience 14*, no. 7 (2013): 488–501.

34. **Our neural activity intensifies:** Julian Q. Kosciessa, Ulman Lindenberger, and Douglas D. Garrett, "Thalamocortical Excitability Modulation Guides Human Perception Under Uncertainty," *Nature Communications 12*, no. 1 (2021): 2430.

34. **uncertainty has been found to cause more stress:** A study (De Berker et al., 2016) found that situations in which subjects had a 50 percent

chance of receiving a shock were more stressful than the ones with 0 percent and 100 percent chances. Archy O. de Berker et al., "Computations of Uncertainty Mediate Acute Stress Responses in Humans," *Nature Communications* 7, no. 1 (2016): 10996.

35. **psychologists call compensatory control:** Mark J. Landau, Aaron C. Kay, and Jennifer A. Whitson, "Compensatory Control and the Appeal of a Structured World," *Psychological Bulletin* 141, no. 3 (2015): 694.

36. **activities that restore our sense of control:** Soo Kim and Derek D. Rucker, "Bracing for the Psychological Storm: Proactive Versus Reactive Compensatory Consumption," *Journal of Consumer Research* 39, no. 4 (2012): 815–30.

36. **freedom lies within the gap:** "Between stimulus and response there is space. In that space is our power to choose our response. In our response lies our growth and our freedom." I have seen this quote attributed to Viktor Frankl, Stephen Covey, and Rollo May, and there doesn't seem to be a clear attribution to this day, although Quote Investigator did a great job at exploring its origins: https://quoteinvestigator.com/2018/02/18/response/.

36. **"the decision to act":** Muriel Earhart Morrissey and Carol L. Osborne, *Amelia, My Courageous Sister: Biography of Amelia Earhart* (Santa Clara, CA: Osborne Publisher, 1987).

CHAPTER 2: ESCAPING THE TYRANNY OF PURPOSE

39. **the phrase *find your purpose*:** Google Ngram Viewer, "Find Your Purpose" (1819–2019).

41. **which psychologists call self-complexity:** Patricia W. Linville, "Self-Complexity and Affective Extremity: Don't Put All of Your Eggs in One Cognitive Basket," *Social Cognition* 3, no. 1 (1985): 94–120.

42. **only one rule of screenwriting:** Jenna Milly, "Podcast: Screenwriter Leslie Dixon Talks *Limitless*," *Script,* March 17, 2011, https://scriptmag.com/features/podcast-screenwriter-leslie-dixon-talks-limitless.

42. **as we mature:** John W. Gardner, "The World Is Your Classroom: Lessons in Self-Renewal," *Futurist* 36, no. 3 (2002): 52–53.

43. **the components of a particular "scene":** Gordon H. Bower, John B. Black, and Terrence J. Turner, "Scripts in Memory for Text," *Cognitive Psychology* 11, no. 2 (1979): 177–220.

43. **Cognitive Script Theory:** Robert P. Abelson, "Psychological Status of the Script Concept," *American Psychologist* 36, no. 7 (1981): 715–29.

43. **the brain attempts to match:** Moshe Bar, "The Proactive Brain: Memory for Predictions," *Philosophical Transactions of the Royal Society B: Biological Sciences* 364, no. 1521 (2009): 1235–43.

45. **Adjusting your decisions:** Mirre Stallen and Alan G. Sanfey, "The Neuroscience of Social Conformity: Implications for Fundamental and Applied Research," *Frontiers in Neuroscience* 9 (2015): 337.

45. **Neuroimaging studies have shown:** K. Richard Ridderinkhof et al., "The Role of the Medial Frontal Cortex in Cognitive Control," *Science* 306, no. 5695 (2004): 443–47.

47. **due to survivorship bias:** Stephen J. Brown et al., "Survivorship Bias in Performance Studies," *Review of Financial Studies* 5, no. 4 (1992): 553–80.

47. **you don't have a clear existing passion:** Cal Newport, *So Good They Can't Ignore You: Why Skills Trump Passion in the Quest for Work You Love* (London: Hachette UK, 2012).

48. **"lead them to put all their eggs in one basket":** Paul A. O'Keefe, Carol S. Dweck, and Gregory M. Walton, "Implicit Theories of Interest: Finding Your Passion or Developing It?," *Psychological Science* 29, no. 10 (2018): 1653–64.

48. **the illiterate of our times:** Alvin Toffler, *Oxford Essential Quotations,* 4th ed., online version, ed. Susan Ratcliffe (Oxford: Oxford University Press, 2016).

48. **In Japanese Noh theater:** This is referred to as 似せぬ (*nisenu*), or non-imitation, which is described by scholars as a form of unlearning, putting down skills, and emptying intention. See Tadashi Nishihira and Jeremy Rappleye, "Unlearning as (Japanese) Learning," *Educational Philosophy and Theory* 54, no. 9 (2022): 1332–44.

49. **The number one barrier to self-renewal:** From a survey of more than a thousand creators and people who want to become creators: Ann Handley et al., Creator Economy Benchmark Research, The Tilt, 2023, https://www.thetilt.com/research.

50. **"The difficulty lies, not in the new ideas":** John Maynard Keynes, *The General Theory of Employment, Interest and Money* (London: Macmillan, 1936).

50. **"the open-mindedness with which one must look and listen":** Margaret Mead, *Sex and Temperament in Three Primitive Societies* (London: Routledge, 1977).

50. **Anthropologists ask fundamental questions:** Devin Proctor, "What Is Cultural Anthropology?," *Sapiens*, September 27, 2022, https://www.sapiens.org/culture/what-is-cultural-anthropology/.

51. **write a time stamp and a few words:** I got the idea for the time stamps from the CEO of *Medium*. It's an easy way to add a layer of helpful data to your field notes. Tony Stubblebine, "Replace Your To-Do List with Interstitial Journaling to Increase Productivity," Medium, September 7, 2017.

51. **The aim is not to create a lengthy narrativized record:** You don't want, of course, to turn into Funes the Memorious, who finds that writing down a full day's worth of memories takes him another full day. From one of my favorite collections of short stories: Jorge Luis Borges, *Labyrinths: Selected Stories and Other Writings,* ed. Donald A. Yates and James E. Irby (New York: New Directions, 1962).

CHAPTER 3: A PACT TO TURN DOUBTS INTO EXPERIMENTS

55. **Alexander Kallaway was once:** Quincy Larson, "The #100DaysOfCode Challenge, Its History, and Why You Should Try It for 2021," *freeCodeCamp,* https://www.freecodecamp.org/news/the-crazy-history -of-the-100daysofcode-challenge-and-why-you-should-try-it-for-2018- 6c89a76e298d/.

57. **The pact is the fundamental building block:** I first formulated the pact as part of a personal growth framework I called mindframing, which is based on four pillars: Pact, Act, React, Impact (PARI means "wager" in my native French). Much of the content and structure of this book is derived and evolved from my early work on mindframing.

59. **"action and feeling go together":** William James, *On Vital Reserves: The Energies of Men; The Gospel of Relaxation* (New York: H. Holt, 1911).

61. **"findings in modern creativity work":** Roger E. Beaty and Paul J. Silvia, "Why Do Ideas Get More Creative Across Time? An Executive Interpretation of the Serial Order Effect in Divergent Thinking Tasks," *Psychology of Aesthetics, Creativity, and the Arts* 6, no. 4 (2012): 309–19.

61. **creativity can be nurtured:** Adam Alter, "How to Be More Creative," *The Atlantic,* May 20, 2023, https://www.theatlantic.com/ideas /archive/2023/05/creativity-persistence-breakthroughs-silicon-valley /674114/#.

61. **the odds of a founder in their fifties:** Pierre Azoulay et al., "Age and High-Growth Entrepreneurship," *American Economic Review: Insights* 2, no. 1 (2020): 65–82.

61. **The peak productivity of a scientist:** R. Bjørk, "The Age at Which Noble Prize Research Is Conducted," *Scientometrics* 119, no. 2 (2019): 931–39.

61. **"The more you do, the more you fail":** John C. Maxwell, *Failing Forward: Turning Mistakes into Stepping Stones for Success* (New York: HarperCollins Leadership, 2007).

62. **Sarah Tate, a former Google colleague:** Sarah shared her experience on LinkedIn when she was ten months in and very much enjoying her work as a coach. Sarah Tate, "A lot of people told me not to launch a coach-

ing business," LinkedIn, February 9, 2024, https://www.linkedin.com /posts/sarah-tate-96b76116_careers-careerstrategy-coachingbusiness -activity-7161614741671501825-3eF3/.

63. **more likely to stick to a habit if it's rewarding:** Gaby Judah et al., "Exploratory Study of the Impact of Perceived Reward on Habit Formation," *BMC Psychology* 6, no. 62 (2018): 1–12.

63. **I started journaling as part of a two-week pact:** This particular pact was part of my preparation for my first ayahuasca ceremony. We were asked to incorporate a mindfulness practice. I wasn't sure which one would work for me, so I experimented with yoga and journaling. Only journaling has turned into a habit.

64. **Strava found that most New Year's resolutions:** *Year in Sport Data Report,* 2017, Strava, Inc., quoted in Sabrina Barr, "Quitters' Day: People Most Likely to Give Up New Year's Resolutions Today," *Independent,* January 12, 2018, https://www.independent.co.uk/life -style/quitters-day-new-years-resolutions-give-up-fail-today-a8155386 .html.

64. **known as the effort paradox:** Michael Inzlicht, Amitai Shenhav, and Christopher Y. Olivola, "The Effort Paradox: Effort Is Both Costly and Valued," *Trends in Cognitive Sciences* 22, no. 4 (2018): 337–49.

66. **The overconfidence effect:** Gerry Pallier et al., "The Role of Individual Differences in the Accuracy of Confidence Judgments," *Journal of General Psychology* 129, no. 3 (2002), 257–99.

66. **the planning fallacy:** Roger Buehler, Dale Griffin, and Michael Ross, "Exploring the 'Planning Fallacy': Why People Underestimate Their Task Completion Times," *Journal of Personality and Social Psychology* 67, no. 3 (1994): 366–81.

66. **actor and writer Henri Brugère:** If you speak French, you can follow Henri's scriptwriting work at @fuseesetautresscripteslibres on Instagram.

67. **Albert Einstein conducted:** *Einstein at the Patent Office,* Swiss Federal Institute of Intellectual Property, https://www.ige.ch/en/about-us/the -history-of-the-ipi/einstein/einstein-at-the-patent-office.

67. **Haruki Murakami wrote his first two books:** Haruki Murakami, *What I Talk About When I Talk About Running: A Memoir* (New York: Vintage Books, 2009).

68. **Tasshin Fogleman makes the distinction:** Tasshin Fogleman, "Tasshin's Talking Points on Love, Curiosity, and Empowerment," *Love Pilgrim,* April 26, 2023, https://tasshin.com/blog/talking-points-2023/.

69. **"choosing what to work on is the highest leverage":** Artur is an AI engineer at Automattic, the company that created WordPress. He enrolled a dozen of his teammates with him in one of my courses. This quote of his is from the 2022 Mindful Productivity Masterclass feedback form.

CHAPTER 4: A DEEPER SENSE OF TIME

74. **the fear of time running out:** Torschlusspanik literally means "gate-shut panic." In the Middle Ages, city gates used to be closed at nightfall, forcing latecomers to stay outside. Today, the expression is used metaphorically to describe the feeling that you may miss out on opportunities if you don't act quickly enough as time passes and the gates close.

74. **The efficiency trap:** Oliver Burkeman, "Escaping the Efficiency Trap—and Finding Some Peace of Mind," *Wall Street Journal*, August 6, 2021, https://www.wsj.com/articles/escaping-the-efficiency-trapand-finding-some-peace-of-mind-11628262751.

75. **being a productive member of society:** See this eloquent overview of productivity culture over the past century: Cal Newport, "The Frustration with Productivity Culture," *The New Yorker*, September 13, 2021, https://www.newyorker.com/culture/office-space/the-frustration-with-productivity-culture.

75. **"all of the economic and social gains of the 20th century":** Peter F. Drucker, "Knowledge-Worker Productivity: The Biggest Challenge," in John A. Woods and James Cortada, eds., *The Knowledge Management Yearbook 2000–2001* (New York: Routledge, 2000), 267–83.

76. **known as monotropism in autism:** Daniel Poole et al., "'No Idea of Time': Parents Report Differences in Autistic Children's Behaviour Relating to Time in a Mixed-Methods Study," *Autism* 25, no. 6 (2021): 1797–808.

76. **and hyperfocus in ADHD:** Kathleen E. Hupfeld, Tessa R. Abagis, and Priti Shah, "Living 'in the Zone': Hyperfocus in Adult ADHD," *ADHD Attention Deficit and Hyperactivity Disorders* 11, no. 2 (2019): 191–208.

77. **two words to speak of time:** Emily Drabinski, "Toward a Kairos of Library Instruction," *Journal of Academic Librarianship* 40, no. 5 (2014): 480–85.

78. **Petrarch talks of this:** Francis Petrarch, *Triumphus Temporis*, ca. 1351–74, trans. Peter Sadlon, petersadlon.com. Reproduced under the website's open-use policy.

79. **Research into time perception:** Peter Ulric Tse et al., "Attention and the Subjective Expansion of Time," *Perception & Psychophysics* 66, no. 7 (2004): 1171–89.

79. **a phenomenon related to Mihaly Csikszentmihalyi's concept of flow:** Jeanne Nakamura and Mihaly Csikszentmihalyi, "The Concept of Flow," in *Handbook of Positive Psychology*, ed. C. R. Snyder and Shane J. Lopez (New York: Oxford University Press, 2002), 90–105.

81. **fiction writer Neal Stephenson explains:** Neal Stephenson, "Why I Am a Bad Correspondent," https://www.nealstephenson.com/why-i-am-a -bad-correspondent.html.

83. **our morning or evening preferences:** Youna Hu et al., "GWAS of 89,283 Individuals Identifies Genetic Variants Associated with Self-Reporting of Being a Morning Person," *Nature Communications* 7, no. 1 (2016): 10448.

83. **what American author Daniel Pink calls:** Daniel H. Pink, *When: The Scientific Secrets of Perfect Timing* (New York: Riverhead, 2019), 44; Till Roenneberg, Anna Wirz-Justice, and Martha Merrow, "Life Between Clocks: Daily Temporal Patterns of Human Chronotypes," *Journal of Biological Rhythms* 18, no. 1 (2003): 80–90; Iwona Chelminski et al., "Horne and Ostberg Questionnaire: A Score Distribution in a Large Sample of Young Adults," *Personality and Individual Differences* 23, no. 4 (1997): 647–52.

84. **the team's players kept track of their periods:** Alisha Haridasani Gupta, "Cycle Syncing Is Trendy. Does It Work?," *New York Times*, June 1, 2023, https://www.nytimes.com/2023/06/01/well/move/menstrual-cycle -syncing-exercise.html.

84. **scoring the team's second goal in a 2–0 victory:** Kieran Pender, "Ending Period 'Taboo' Gave the USA a Marginal Gain at the World Cup," *The Telegraph*, July 13, 2019.

84. **circannual cycles:** Christelle Meyer et al., "Seasonality in Human Cognitive Brain Responses," *Proceedings of the National Academy of Sciences* 113, no. 11 (2016): 3066–71.

84. **Winston Churchill took naps during the day:** Joseph Cardieri, "Churchill Understood Afternoon Naps," *New York Times*, October 2, 1989, https://www.nytimes.com/1989/10/02/opinion/l-churchill-understood -afternoon-naps-838589.html.

85. **"Live in each season as it passes":** Henry David Thoreau, *The Thoughts of Thoreau*, selected by Edwin Way Teale (New York: Dodd, Mead, 1962).

85. **like investor and entrepreneur Sahil Bloom:** Sahil Bloom, "Ultimate Calendar Hack, How to Negotiate, and More," *The Friday Five*, July 1, 2022, https://www.sahilbloom.com/newsletter/energy-calendars-how-to -negotiate-more.

87. **our performance drops dramatically:** Kevin P. Madore and Anthony D. Wagner, "Multicosts of Multitasking," *Cerebrum: The Dana Forum on Brain Science* (2019).

87. **an attentional bottleneck:** Michael N. Tombu et al., "A Unified Attentional Bottleneck in the Human Brain," *Proceedings of the National Academy of Sciences* 108, no. 33 (2011): 13426–31.

87. **"one area where we are seriously limited is working memory"**: Bill Cerbin, "Working Memory as a Bottleneck in Learning," Exploring How Students Learn, 2008; uploaded as "Working Memory and Cognitive Overload" on November 8, 2019, at https://takinglearningseriously.com/2019/11/08/working-memory-and-cognitive-overload/.

88. **"There's no such thing as not in the mood"**: "Madonna Unveils Her Tour Movie," *Irish Independent,* June 20, 2013, https://www.independent.ie/style/celebrity/madonna-unveils-her-tour-movie/29359765.html.

89. **known as eustress, which means "good stress" in Greek**: Matthew Blake Hargrove, Debra L. Nelson, and Cary L. Cooper, "Generating Eustress by Challenging Employees: Helping People Savor Their Work," *Organizational Dynamics* 42, no. 1 (2013): 61–69.

89. **like a sandpile growing increasingly unstable**: This is a phenomenon known as self-organized criticality in science. Per Bak, Chao Tang, and Kurt Wiesenfeld, "Self-Organized Criticality: An Explanation of the 1/f Noise," *Physical Review Letters* 59, no. 4 (1987), 381.

89. **a phenomenon psychologists refer to as free-floating anxiety**: "Free-Floating Anxiety," *APA Dictionary of Psychology*, updated April 19, 2018, https://dictionary.apa.org/free-floating-anxiety.

90. **Moving your body has been found to relieve anxiety straightaway**: Felipe B. Schuch et al., "Physical Activity Protects from Incident Anxiety: A Meta-Analysis of Prospective Cohort Studies," *Depression and Anxiety* 36, no. 9 (2019), 846–58.

90. **to create a virtuous cycle**: Michel Audiffren and Nathalie André, "The Exercise–Cognition Relationship: A Virtuous Circle," *Journal of Sport and Health Science* 8, no. 4 (2019), 339–47.

90. **Pay attention to the sensations in your stomach**: This ability to pay attention to your inner sensations is called interoceptive awareness. I wrote an article explaining how it works: Anne-Laure Le Cunff, "Interoception: The Hidden 'Sixth Sense,'" *Ness Labs* (blog), August 21, 2023, https://nesslabs.com/interoception.

90. **focus on the inner experience of the movement**: Julie A. Brodie and Elin E. Lobel, *Dance and Somatics: Mind-Body Principles of Teaching and Performance* (Jefferson, NC: McFarland, 2012).

90. **what Susan David calls emotional agility**: Susan A. David, *Emotional Agility: Get Unstuck, Embrace Change, and Thrive in Work and Life* (New York: Avery, 2016).

CHAPTER 5: PROCRASTINATION IS NOT THE ENEMY

97. **Victor Hugo asked his staff**: Madame Hugo [Adèle Foucher], *Victor Hugo by a Witness of His Life* (New York: Carleton, 1863).

98. **"wasted the cream of my brain on the telephone":** Virginia Woolf, *The Diary of Virginia Woolf, Vol. 2: 1920–24* (London: Granta Books, 2023).

98. **"Do not put your work off till tomorrow":** Hesiod (c. 700 BC), *Works and Days*, line 410, Perseus Digital Library Project.

99. **As in the teachings of the Buddha:** Valentina Nicolardi et al., "The Two Arrows of Pain: Mechanisms of Pain Related to Meditation and Mental States of Aversion and Identification," *Mindfulness* 15 (2024): 753–74.

99. **said Dr. Tim Pychyl:** Ali Abdaal, "World's Leading Expert on How to Solve Procrastination—Dr. Tim Pychyl," August 25, 2022, YouTube video, 1:21:08, https://www.youtube.com/watch?v=dGIUtVu7w4Y.

100. **a weakened connection between:** Zhiyi Chen et al., "Neural Markers of Procrastination in White Matter Microstructures and Networks," *Psychophysiology* 58, no. 5 (2021): e13782.

100. **a battle between the present self and the future self:** This is unfortunately something I see happening time and time again in recent neuroscientific research, where the role of emotions is minimized or even completely discarded. See, for instance, Raphaël Le Bouc and Mathias Pessiglione, "A Neuro-Computational Account of Procrastination Behavior," *Nature Communications* 13, no. 1 (2022): 5639.

103. **"Should is a shame-based statement":** Susanna Newsonen, "Why No Good Comes from the Word 'Should,'" *Psychology Today* (blog), May 30, 2022.

104. **Clue offers hundreds of permutations:** According to the Strong National Museum of Play, the game offers exactly 324 different murder scenario combinations, which means the game plays differently almost every time.

104. **it forever changed his career path:** Henry Barnard, ed., *Pestalozzi and Pestalozzianism: Life, Educational Principles, and Methods of Johann Heinrich Pestalozzi* (New York: F. C. Brownell, 1859).

104. **Convinced that education should be available to all:** John Alfred Green, *The Educational Ideas of Pestalozzi* (London: W. B. Clive, 1905).

104. **education was often reserved for the wealthy:** Auguste Pinloche, *Pestalozzi and the Foundation of the Modern Elementary School* (New York: Charles Scribner's Sons, 1901).

104. **"Learning by head, hand, and heart":** Whether Pestalozzi used this exact motto is unclear, but he used similar wording in an 1805 essay titled "Pädagogische Auseinandersetzung mit Pfarrer Karl Witte," in his *Sämtliche Werke* (1973), vol. 17A (141–76). The origin of the motto is further discussed in Rebekka Horlacher, "Vocational and Liberal Education in Pestalozzi's Educational Theory," *Pedagogía y Saberes* 50 (2019): 109–20.

105. **human motivation arises from the interplay:** Hugo M. Kehr, "Integrating Implicit Motives, Explicit Motives, and Perceived Abilities: The Compensatory Model of Work Motivation and Volition," *Academy of Management Review* 29, no. 3 (2004), 479–99.

107. **"I needed a different style of newsletter":** Interintellect, "James Clear: Tiny Changes, Remarkable Results," with Anne-Laure Le Cunff, edited by Anna Gát, January 27, 2023, YouTube video, 1:27:52, https://www.youtube.com/watch?v=HGDMEcCHbUY.

109. **what behavioral scientists call a pairing method:** While pairing is often associated with classical conditioning, pairing methods are found in many areas of behavioral science, where it is also known as behavioral coupling or temptation bundling. Dr. Hannah Rose wrote a short guide on Ness Labs: https://nesslabs.com/temptation-bundling.

CHAPTER 6: THE POWER OF INTENTIONAL IMPERFECTION

115. **Shonda Rhimes's career:** Shonda Rhimes, *Year of Yes: How to Dance It Out, Stand in the Sun and Be Your Own Person* (New York: Simon & Schuster, 2015).

116. **"If I am excelling at one thing":** Judy Berman, "Shonda Rhimes Already Knows What You're Going to Watch Next," *Time*, January 10, 2022, https://time.com/6132884/shonda-rhimes-profile/.

117. **"nothing is perfect":** One of my very few regrets in life is to have missed an opportunity to meet with Stephen Hawking when I was still working at Google. I read all his books as a kid and was a massive fan. This quote appeared in a Google Doodle posthumously celebrating Stephen Hawking's eightieth birthday. "In the Doodle, the voice of Stephen Hawking was generated and used with the approval of the Hawking estate," the announcement explains: https://doodles.google/doodle/stephen-hawkings-80th-birthday/.

117. **philosopher Gloria Origgi and sociology professor Diego Gambetta:** Manuela Saragosa, "How to Be Mediocre and Be Happy with Yourself," *BBC News*, August 22, 2016, https://www.bbc.com/news/business-37108240.

118. **"a common appreciation of the Italian laid-back way of life?":** Diego Gambetta and Gloria Origgi, "The LL Game: The Curious Preference for Low Quality and Its Norms," *Politics, Philosophy & Economics* 12, no. 1 (2013): 3–23.

118. **the *dolce vita*—"the sweet life":** Maria L. Kimmerle, *La Dolce Vita, the Italian Case Study: Linking Culture, Policy and "Active Aging"* (global honors thesis, University of Washington Tacoma, 2013) https://digitalcommons.tacoma.uw.edu/gh_theses/12/.

118. **Italy is also known for its world-class excellence:** Serena Rovai and Manuela De Carlo, eds., *Made in Italy and the Luxury Market: Heritage, Sustainability and Innovation* (London: Routledge, 2023).

118. **Italy's public healthcare system:** Francesca Ferré et al., "Italy: Health System Review," World Health Organization, *Health Systems in Transition* 16, no. 4 (2014): 1-168, https://iris.who.int/bitstream/handle /10665/141626/HiT-16-4-2014-eng.pdf?sequence=5&isAllowed=y.

119. **Italy's postal service:** Gabriella Romani, *Postal Culture: Writing and Reading Letters in Post-Unification Italy* (Toronto: University of Toronto Press, 2013).

119. **Italy's fashion industry:** Italian Fashion Chamber, "Statistiche della moda Italia," Confidustria Moda, 2018.

119. **a robust technological sector:** M. Bugamelli et al., "Productivity Growth in Italy: A Tale of a Slow-Motion Change," Banca d'Italia Eurosistema, *Questioni di Economia e Finanza* 422 (January 2018).

119. **the greatest perfection lies in imperfection:** Władysław Tatarkiewicz and Christopher Kasparek, "Paradoxes of Perfection," *Dialectics and Humanism* 7, no. 1 (1980): 77–80.

119. **Vanini, who considered himself a freethinker:** Lucilio Vanini was one of the first modern thinkers to regard the universe as an entity governed by natural laws, and he was an early advocate of biological evolution, arguing that humans and other apes have common ancestors. His tongue was cut out and he was executed for these ideas.

120. **we become able to manage stress better:** Steven M. Southwick and Dennis S. Charney, *Resilience: The Science of Mastering Life's Greatest Challenges* (New York: Cambridge University Press, 2018).

120. **Trosky shared the counterintuitive strategy:** Mary Childs, "Former Bond Manager Shares Investing Strategy That He Calls Strategic Mediocrity," NPR, June 3, 2022, https://www.npr.org/2022/06/03/11028 41155/former-bond-manager-shares-investing-strategy-that-he-calls -strategic-mediocrity.

120. *strategic mediocrity*: Childs, "Former Bond Manager Shares Investing Strategy That He Calls Strategic Mediocrity."

121. **the following observation on Twitter:** Bowser, X (formerly Twitter), August 11, 2023, https://twitter.com/browserdotsys/status/1689957766 415237121 (tweet since deleted).

122. **You've got to put down the ducky:** Josh Green, "Muppets Gone Missing: Norman Stiles," *Graphic Policy*, July 16, 2015.

122. **joining the 50 percent of candidates:** Robin Wollast et al., "Who Are the Doctoral Students Who Drop Out? Factors Associated with the Rate of Doctoral Degree Completion in Universities," *International Journal of Higher Education* 7, no. 4 (2018): 143–56.

123. **like other founders who "work like hell"**: "Work like hell. I mean you just have to put in 80- to 100-hour weeks every week. . . . If other people are putting in 40-hour workweeks and you're putting in 100-hour workweeks, then even if you're doing the same thing, you know that you will achieve in four months what it takes them a year to achieve" is advice given by Elon Musk during an interview with Bambi Francisco Roizen, the founder of Vator, a media and research firm for entrepreneurs and investors. See https://vator.tv/n/152d.

125. **"An error in an artwork"**: Cedric van Eenoo, "The Art of Making Mistakes," *International Journal of Arts* 2, no. 3 (2012): 7–10.

CHAPTER 7: CREATING GROWTH LOOPS

129. **In an interview with *Outside***: Cathal Dennehy, "The Surprisingly Simple Training of the World's Fastest Marathoner," *Outside*, July 5, 2023.

130. **As Nassim Taleb has put it**: Nassim Nicholas Taleb, "Understanding Is a Poor Substitute for Convexity (Antifragility)," Edge Foundation, December 12, 2012, https://www.edge.org/conversation/nassim _nicholas_taleb-understanding-is-a-poor-substitute-for-convexity -antifragility.

130. **Nature adapts in response to environmental feedback**: Scientists are now playing with these cycles of experimentation in the laboratory. See Michael J. McDonald, "Microbial Experimental Evolution—A Proving Ground for Evolutionary Theory and a Tool for Discovery," *EMBO Reports* 20, no. 8 (2019): e46992.

131. **make small adjustments each time**: P. M. Rabbitt, "Errors and Error Correction in Choice-Response Tasks," *Journal of Experimental Psychology* 71, no. 2 (1966): 264–72.

131. **the wheel is a symbol of growth**: Raffaele Pettazzoni, "The Wheel in the Ritual Symbolism of Some Indo-European Peoples," in *Essays on the History of Religions* (Leiden: Brill, 1954), 95–109.

131. **the desire to find balance**: Paul Downes, "Concentric and Diametric Structures in Yin/Yang and the Mandala Symbol: A New Wave of Eastern Frames for Psychology," *Psychology and Developing Societies* 23, no. 1 (2011): 121–53.

131. **the phoenix cyclically regenerates**: Sister Mary Francis McDonald, "Phoenix Redivivus," *Phoenix* 14, no. 4 (1960): 187–206.

131. **built on a giant perception-action cycle**: Joaquín M. Fuster, "Physiology of Executive Functions: The Perception-Action Cycle," *Principles of Frontal Lobe Function*, ed. Donald T. Stuss and Robert T. Knight (New York: Oxford University Press, 2002), 96–108.

131. **the theoretical cornerstone of most modern theories of learning:** Marta I. Garrido et al., "Evoked Brain Responses Are Generated by Feedback Loops," *Proceedings of the National Academy of Sciences* 104, no. 52 (2007): 20961–66.

132. **their signature "tiki-taka" style of play:** Hans-Joachim Braun, "Soccer Tactics as Science? On 'Scotch Professors,' a Ukrainian Soccer Buddha, and a Catalonian Who Tries to Learn German," *Icon* 19 (2013): 216–43.

132. **"you can fix it":** Lydia Belanger, "17 Inspirational Quotes from Master Chef Julia Child," *Entrepreneur*, August 15, 2016, https://www.entrepreneur.com/leadership/17-inspirational-quotes-from-master-chef-julia-child/280869.

133. **without metacognition:** Damien S. Fleur, Bert Bredeweg, and Wouter van den Bos, "Metacognition: Ideas and Insights from Neuro- and Educational Sciences," *npj Science of Learning* 6, no. 1 (2021): 13.

134. **Consider Barbara Oakley:** Barbara Oakley, *A Mind for Numbers: How to Excel at Math and Science (Even If You Flunked Algebra)* (New York: Penguin, 2014).

134. **balance times of intense concentration (focused mode):** Making space for the diffuse mode of thinking is one of my favorite metacognitive strategies of hers (maybe half of the aha moments for this book I had in the shower or while absent-mindedly cutting vegetables) and has since been backed by extensive neuroscientific research into the default mode network. See Marcus E. Raichle, "The Brain's Default Mode Network," *Annual Review of Neuroscience* 38 (2015): 433–47.

134. **Metacognition is for good reason often referred to:** Stephen M. Fleming, "Metacognition Is the Forgotten Secret to Success," *Scientific American*, September 1, 2014, https://www.scientificamerican.com/article/metacognition-is-the-forgotten-secret-to-success/.

139. **reflection in action:** Peter J. Collier and Dilafruz R. Williams, "Reflection in Action: The Learning-Doing Relationship," in *Learning Through Serving: A Student Guidebook for Service-Learning Across Disciplines*, ed. Christine M. Cress, Peter J. Collier, and Vicki L. Reitenauer (New York: Routledge, 2005), 95–111.

140. **"begin to think multidimensionally":** M. Scott Peck, *The Road Less Traveled* (New York: Simon & Schuster, 1978).

141. **whether you use bullet journaling:** The bullet journal, invented by Ryder Carroll, often serves as a combined space for reflection, planning, and tracking, and the visual format of Plus Minus Next works great with bullet journaling. You can use different colors for the symbols and adapt the design of the columns to suit the style of your journal. See A. Luzong, "What Is the Bullet Journal Method?," *Bullet Journal*, De-

cember 14, 2023, https://bulletjournal.com/blogs/faq/what-is-the-bullet-journal-method.

141. **morning pages:** Morning pages, as described by Julia Cameron in *The Artist's Way*, involves writing three pages of longhand, stream-of-consciousness writing first thing in the morning. After completing your morning pages, you could take some time to review what you've written and identify any positive observations, challenges, and potential plans for the future, then succinctly capture these in your Plus Minus Next columns. See Julia Cameron, "The Bedrock Tool of the Artist's Way: Morning Pages," *The Artist's Way*, September 24, 2019, https://juliacameronlive.com/2019/09/24/the-bedrock-tool-of-the-artists-way-morning-pages/.

143. **he would start sketching ideas without a full understanding:** Rachel Wintemberg, "On Messing Up, Trial, Error and the Creative Process," *The Helpful Art Teacher* (blog), April 17, 2016.

143. **his inky fingerprints have been used:** Martin Bailey, "Leonardo da Vinci's Thumbprint Discovered on Drawing in the Royal Collection," *The Art Newspaper*, January 28, 2019.

143. **To err is human:** Often attributed to Seneca the Younger: *Errare humanum est, perseverare autem diabolicum* ("To err is human, but to persist is diabolical"). But I prefer this version: *Errare humanum est, in errore perseverare stultum* ("To err is human, but to persist in error is foolish").

143. **strive to make good mistakes:** Daniel C. Dennett, "Making Mistakes," in *Intuition Pumps and Other Tools for Thinking* (New York: W. W. Norton, 2013), 19–28.

CHAPTER 8: THE SECRET TO BETTER DECISIONS

149. **decision-making can be irrationally driven:** Benedetto De Martino et al., "Frames, Biases, and Rational Decision-Making in the Human Brain," *Science* 313, no. 5787 (2006): 684–87.

150. **In many indigenous societies around the world:** Fulvio Mazzocchi, "A Deeper Meaning of Sustainability: Insights from Indigenous Knowledge," *Anthropocene Review* 7, no. 1 (2020): 77–93.

150. **In medieval guilds:** George François Renard, *Guilds in the Middle Ages*, translated by Dorothy Terry and edited with an introduction by G. D. H. Cole (London: G. Bell and Sons, 1919).

150. **many Asian philosophies emphasize the importance of balance:** Peter Ping Li, "The Epistemology of Yin-Yang Balancing as the Root of Chinese Cultural Traditions: The Indigenous Features and Geocentric Implications," in *The Psychological and Cultural Foundations of East*

Asian Cognition: Contradiction, Change, and Holism, ed. Julie Spencer-Rodgers and Kaiping Peng (New York: Oxford University Press, 2018), 35–79.

151. **Maria Popova, who has been writing weekly essays:** Formerly known as *Brain Pickings*: https://www.themarginalian.org/2021/10/22/brain -pickings-becoming-the-marginalian/.

151. **on the night Gautama Buddha was conceived:** "Maha Maya, Mother of Gautama Buddha," in *Encyclopedia Britannica*, https://www.bri tannica.com/biography/Maha-Maya.

151. **beautiful but useless possession:** "white elephant," in *Oxford Dictionaries*: "A possession that is useless or troublesome, especially one that is expensive to maintain or difficult to dispose of."

152. **an absurd escalation of commitment:** *Escalation of commitment* is a term used in psychology to describe situations where people maintain irrational behaviors because they align with previous decisions and actions. Dustin J. Sleesman et al., "Putting Escalation of Commitment in Context: A Multilevel Review and Analysis," *Academy of Management Annals* 12, no. 1 (2018): 178–207.

152. **"Quitting the projects that don't go anywhere":** Seth Godin, *The Dip: A Little Book That Teaches You When to Quit (and When to Stick)* (New York: Portfolio, 2007).

153. **I successfully completed my pact:** Through this second pact, I discovered that I didn't want to become a YouTuber. I still occasionally upload videos whenever I find that a topic would work well in this format, but I'm not committed to a weekly cadence anymore.

153. **Watterson said he intended to work:** D. D. Degg, "Parsing Bill Watterson's Farewell Letter," *The Daily Cartoonist*, November 7, 2021.

153. **The final strip ran on December 31, 1995:** Bill Watterson, *The Complete Calvin and Hobbes*, vol. 3 (Kansas City, MO: Andrews McMeel, 2012), 481. Comic originally published December 31, 1995.

155. **Known as the Honda Point disaster:** Frankie Witzenburg, "Disaster at Honda Point: The U.S. Navy's Largest Peacetime Loss of Ships," *Naval History Magazine* 34, no. 5 (2020), https://www.usni.org/magazines /naval-history-magazine/2020/october/disaster-honda-point.

155. **"he narrowed his cone of uncertainty":** Paul Saffo, "Embracing Uncertainty: The Secret to Effective Forecasting," Long Now Foundation, April 19, 2020, YouTube video, 51:55, https://www.youtube.com/watch ?v=_vp9Dv7Jobw.

157. **What researchers call a narrow decision frame:** Richard P. Larrick, "Broaden the Decision Frame to Make Effective Decisions, in *Handbook of Principles of Organizational Behavior: Indispensable Knowl-*

edge for Evidence-Based Management, ed. Edwin A. Locke (Wiley Online Library, 2012), 461–80.

157. **Even Benjamin Franklin advocated:** Steven Johnson, *Farsighted: How We Make the Decisions That Matter the Most* (New York: Penguin, 2018). Discovered via Maria Popova, "How to Make Difficult Decisions: Benjamin Franklin's Pioneering Pros and Cons Framework," *The Marginalian*, November 14, 2018.

158. **Social psychologist Timothy D. Wilson warns:** Timothy D. Wilson, "Introspection and Self-Narratives," in *Strangers to Ourselves: Discovering the Adaptive Unconscious* (Cambridge, MA: Belknap Press of Harvard University Press, 2002), 159–80.

CHAPTER 9: HOW TO DANCE WITH DISRUPTION

161. **a farmer's horse ran away into the wild:** Paraphrased from Alan Watts, *Eastern Wisdom, Modern Life: Collected Talks: 1960–1969* (Novato, CA: New World Library, 2006).

162. **Founding a groundbreaking software company:** See Michael Singer's website for a biography and complete bibliography: https://untethered soul.com/.

163. **"to separate forcibly, to break apart":** *Oxford English Dictionary* (London: Oxford University Press, 1896).

163. **The stress caused by disruptions:** T. H. Holmes and R. H. Rahe, "The Social Readjustment Rating Scale," *Journal of Psychosomatic Research* 11, no. 2 (1967): 213–18.

163. **Even joyful occasions such as weddings and holidays:** Sheldon Cohen, Michael L. M. Murphy, and Aric A. Prather, "Ten Surprising Facts About Stressful Life Events and Disease Risk," *Annual Review of Psychology* 70 (2019): 577–97.

163. **Any disruption that derails these plans:** C. S. Carver and M. F. Scheier, "Stress, Coping, and Self-Regulatory Processes," in *Handbook of Personality*, ed. Lawrence A. Pervin and Oliver P. John (New York: Guilford Press, 1999), 553–75.

163. **Disruptive life events and personal stressors:** Akbar Hassanzadeh et al., "Association of Stressful Life Events with Psychological Problems: A Large-Scale Community-Based Study Using Grouped Outcomes Latent Factor Regression with Latent Predictors," *Computational and Mathematical Methods in Medicine*, 2017 (2017): 3457103.

163. **disruptive life events play more of a role:** See this interview with Professor Peter Kinderman, head of the Institute of Psychology, Health and Society at the University of Liverpool: Sarah Knapton, "Mental Illness Mostly Caused by Life Events Not Genetics, Argue Psychologists," *The Telegraph*, March 28, 2016, https://www.telegraph.co.uk/news/2016

/03/28/mental-illness-mostly-caused-by-life-events-not-genetics
-argue-p/.

164. **Buddhism teaches that suffering:** John Peacock, "Suffering in Mind: The Aetiology of Suffering in Early Buddhism," *Contemporary Buddhism* 9, no. 2 (2008): 209–26.

164. **Taoism talks about *wu wei*:** Edward Slingerland, "Effortless Action: The Chinese Spiritual Ideal of Wu-wei," *Journal of the American Academy of Religion* 68, no. 2 (2000): 293–328.

164. **In Hindu philosophy, *vairagya* is the detachment:** Georg Feuerstein, "Wisdom: The Hindu Experience and Perspective," in *The World's Great Wisdom: Timeless Teachings from Religions and Philosophies*, ed. Roger Walsh (Albany: State University of New York Press, 2014), 87–108.

164. **Western science is catching up:** Tapas Kumar Aich, "Buddha Philosophy and Western Psychology," *Indian Journal of Psychiatry* 55, suppl. 2 (2013): S165–S170.

164. **One of the hallmarks of psychological well-being:** Shahram Mohammadkhani et al., "Emotional Schemas and Psychological Distress: Mediating Role of Resilience and Cognitive Flexibility," *Iranian Journal of Psychiatry* 17, no. 3 (2022): 284–93.

164. **"Active acceptance means acknowledging a negative, difficult situation":** Yuka Maya Nakamura and Ulrich Orth, "Acceptance as a Coping Reaction: Adaptive or Not?," *Swiss Journal of Psychology* 64, no. 4 (2005): 281–92.

165. **"Life isn't about waiting":** M. Couzin, "Interview with Vivian Greene on Learning to Dance in the Rain and More," *People of Play*, February 13, 2017, https://www.chitag.com/single-post/2017/02/13/interview -with-vivian-greene.

165. **Cultivating a state of calm regardless of external circumstances:** John M. Rist, "The Stoic Concept of Detachment," in *The Stoics*, ed. John M. Rist (Berkeley: University of California Press, 1978), 259–72.

166. **modern forms of therapy consist:** Frank M. Dattilio, "Cognitive-Behavioral Strategies," in *Brief Therapy with Individuals and Couples*, ed. Jon Carlson and Len Sperry (Phoenix, AZ: Zeig, Tucker & Theisen, 2000), 33–70.

166. **Michael Singer arrived at the same conclusion:** Michael A. Singer, *The Surrender Experiment: My Journey into Life's Perfection* (London: Yellow Kite Books, 2015), 65.

166. **negative emotions that are not properly processed:** Jennifer S. Lerner et al., "Emotion and Decision Making," *Annual Review of Psychology* 66 (2015): 799–823.

166. **Uncomfortable emotions are not inherently bad:** Melinda Wenner Moyer, "Lean Into Negative Emotions. It's the Healthy Thing to Do,"

New York Times, April 21, 2023, https://www.nytimes.com/2023/04/21/well/mind/negative-emotions-mental-health.html.

166. **It's how we interpret our emotions:** Emily C. Willroth et al., "Judging Emotions as Good or Bad: Individual Differences and Associations with Psychological Health," *Emotion* 23, no. 7 (2023): 1876–90.

167. **It also reduces activity in the amygdala:** Matthew D. Lieberman et al., "Putting Feelings into Words: Affect Labeling Disrupts Amygdala Activity in Response to Affective Stimuli," *Psychological Science* 18, no. 5 (2007): 421–28.

167. **labeling our emotions relieves our brains:** Hayley Phelan, "What's All This About Journaling?," *New York Times*, October 25, 2018, https://www.nytimes.com/2018/10/25/style/journaling-benefits.html.

168. **emotional states are closely related to landscapes:** Linda Mealey and Peter Theis, "The Relationship Between Mood and Preferences Among Natural Landscapes: An Evolutionary Perspective," *Ethology and Sociobiology* 16, no. 3 (1995): 247–56.

168. **it persists in front of painted landscapes:** Jim Young Jeong, "Emotional Landscapes," (master's thesis, CUNY Hunter College, 2023), https://academicworks.cuny.edu/cgi/viewcontent.cgi?article=2036&context=hc_sas_etds.

168. **To unravel the potential consequences of an event:** URBAN-NET analyzes what-if scenarios and their propagation of effects within and across CISs using consequence cascade models based on the topology of the network. Sangkeun Lee et al., "URBAN-NET: A Network-Based Infrastructure Monitoring and Analysis System for Emergency Management and Public Safety," in *2016 IEEE International Conference on Big Data*, 2600–609.

169. **Assessing the significance of a stressor:** See the vast amount of research on cognitive appraisal, starting with Richard Lazarus and Susan Folkman, *Stress, Appraisal, and Coping* (New York: Springer, 1984). Also a more recent meta-analysis of threat assessment in medical environments: John vonRosenberg, "Cognitive Appraisal and Stress Performance: The Threat/Challenge Matrix and Its Implications on Performance," *Air Medical Journal* 38, no. 5 (2019): 331–33.

171. **"It was a musical thing":** Alan Watts, "Coincidence of Opposites," 1972, Essential Lectures Collection; see transcript at https://www.organism.earth/library/document/tao-of-philosophy-3.

CHAPTER 10: HOW TO UNLOCK SOCIAL FLOW

175. **tapping into shared knowledge:** Diego A. Reinero, Suzanne Dikker, and Jay J. Van Bavel, "Inter-Brain Synchrony in Teams Predicts Collec-

tive Performance," *Social Cognitive and Affective Neuroscience* 16, no.1–2 (2021): 43–57.

176. **Chamber music players are more likely:** Arvid J. Bloom and Paula Skutnick-Henley, "Facilitating Flow Experiences Among Musicians," *American Music Teacher* 54, no. 5 (2005): 24–28.

176. **athletes can more readily experience personal flow states:** Fabian Pels, Jens Kleinert, and Florian Mennigen, "Group Flow: A Scoping Review of Definitions, Theoretical Approaches, Measures and Findings," *PloS One* 13, no.12 (2018): e0210117.

176. **the intrinsic reward of shared focus:** Charles J. Walker, "Experiencing Flow: Is Doing It Together Better Than Doing It Alone?," *Journal of Positive Psychology* 5, no. 1 (2010): 3–11.

176. **This scene gave Monet and Renoir:** "Impressionism and Paris Cafes," *ImpressionistArts*, https://impressionistarts.com/impressionism-cafes -paris.

176. **In Vienna, salons provided Freud:** David S. Luft, "Science and Irrationalism in Freud's Vienna," *Modern Austrian Literature* 23, no. 2 (1990): 89–97.

176. **the Algonquin Round Table in New York:** Dorothy Herrmann, *With Malice Toward All: The Quips, Lives and Loves of Some Celebrated 20th-Century American Wits* (New York: Putnam, 1982), 17–18.

177. **The Bloomsbury Group:** Seyedeh Zahra Nozen, Bahman Amani, and Fatemeh Ziyarat, "Blooming of the Novel in the Bloomsbury Group: An Investigation to the Impact of the Members of Bloomsbury Group on the Composition of the Selected Works of Virginia Woolf and E. M. Forster," *International Journal of Applied Linguistics and English Literature* 6, no. 7 (2017): 323–31.

177. **What collectors call the provenance of a work:** Robin Sutton Anders, "What Is Provenance—and Why Every Art Collector Should Care About It," *Veranda*, August 3, 2023, https://www.veranda.com/luxury -lifestyle/artwork/a44691992/what-is-provenance/#.

178. **none of us can flourish on our own:** Long before there were social network researchers, success was understood as interdependent by ancient philosophies from all around the globe. The African philosophy of Ubuntu ("I am because we are") emphasizes our interconnectedness, stating that individual success is bound to the success of others. "The solitary human being is a contradiction in terms," explained human rights activist Desmond Tutu. Participating, sharing, and belonging are what make us humans. Confucianism shares this view, in which personal success is inseparable from communal harmony through the fulfillment of work that benefits the community as a whole. The San-

gha ("assembly" in Sanskrit), one of Buddhism's three jewels alongside the Buddha and the Dharma, underscores the necessity of a nurturing community for individual success on the path to enlightenment.

178. **continues to romanticize the lone hero:** Alfonso Montuori and Ronald E. Purser, "Deconstructing the Lone Genius Myth: Toward a Contextual View of Creativity," *Journal of Humanistic Psychology* 35, no. 3 (Summer 1995): 69–112.

178. **Each of these individuals contributed pieces to a puzzle:** Such collective intelligence is actually found not just in humans, but at all levels of life. Patrick McMillen and Michael Levin, "Collective Intelligence: A Unifying Concept for Integrating Biology Across Scales and Substrates," *Communications Biology* 7, no. 1 (2024): 378.

179. **Psychologists call this transactive memory:** Daniel M. Wegner, "Transactive Memory: A Contemporary Analysis of the Group Mind," in *Theories of Group Behavior*, ed. Brian Mullen and George R. Goethals (New York: Springer, 1987), 185–208.

180. **it was acquired by Stripe:** Joel Hooks, "How Courtland Allen Grew Indie Hackers with Content, Consistency, and Community" (Episode 66), podcast, February 28, 2020, https://egghead.io/podcasts/how-courtland-allen-found-freedom-with-content-consistency-and-community. In March of 2023, Courtland and Channing spun Indie Hackers back out as an independent business, with Stripe as an investor.

180. **information exchange is the most popular reason:** Catherine M. Ridings and David Gefen, "Virtual Community Attraction: Why People Hang Out Online," *Journal of Computer-Mediated Communication* 10, no. 1 (2004): JCMC10110.

181. **what researchers call communities of practice:** Igor Pyrko, Viktor Dörfler, and Colin Eden, "Thinking Together: What Makes Communities of Practice Work?," *Human Relations* 70, no. 4 (2017): 389–409.

183. **being part of a community improves:** Camilla A. Michalski et al., "Relationship Between Sense of Community Belonging and Self-Rated Health Across Life Stages," *SSM-Population Health* 12 (2020): 100676. See also Kenneth M. Cramer and Hailey Pawsey, "Happiness and Sense of Community Belonging in the World Value Survey," *Current Research in Ecological and Social Psychology* 4 (2023): 100101.

185. **The Rebel Book Club started:** Laura Hampson, "Inside Instagram's Coolest Book Club," *Evening Standard* (London), August 31, 2020, https://www.standard.co.uk/culture/books/rebel-book-club-founders-interview-a4533271.html.

185. **Derrick Downey Jr. started posting videos:** As someone who also feeds the squirrels that visit my balcony (note: almonds are fine, but never feed Brazil nuts to squirrels, as many of them have a selenium intoler-

ance), I'm a big fan of Derrick's account. You can follow him at @derrick downeyjr on Instagram.

186. *Jugaad*, **a Hindi term for innovative problem-solving:** Jaideep Prabhu and Sanjay Jain, "Innovation and Entrepreneurship in India: Understanding Jugaad," *Asia Pacific Journal of Management* 32 (2015): 843–68.

187. **deeper relationships through self-disclosure:** Irwin Altman and Dalmas A. Taylor, *Social Penetration: The Development of Interpersonal Relationships* (New York: Holt, Rinehart & Winston, 1973).

188. **People who are action-oriented tend to thrive:** B. H. McCoy, "Applying the Art of Action-Oriented Decision Making to the Knotty Issues of Everyday Business Life," *Management Review* 72, no. 7 (1983).

188. **Carl Martin immediately felt at home:** "Folkestone Fellas—Minding Men's Mental Health," *Folkelife*, December 8, 2023, https://folke.life /folkestone/live/people-and-stories/folkestone-fellas/.

189. **Fostering psychological safety:** Alexander Newman, Ross Donohue, and Nathan Eva, "Psychological Safety: A Systematic Review of the Literature," *Human Resource Management Review* 27, no. 3 (2017): 521–35.

189. **This creates ambient belonging:** S. A. Hotchkiss et al., "Do I Belong in a Makerspace?: Investigating Student Belonging and Non-Verbal Cues in a University Makerspace," June 2019, in 2019 ASEE Annual Conference & Exposition.

189. **When people feel at home:** A great example of this is The Commons in San Francisco, where I have hosted one of our Ness Labs meetups. Its cofounder Patricia Mou describes it as a "fourth place," or a community for meaning-making encouraging informed self-expression through shared contexts and safe containers: Patricia Mou, "Introducing 'the Fourth Place' & Why 'Third Places' Have Fallen Short on Their Promise," Patricia Mou (website) September 7, 2020, https://www .patriciamou.com/newsletter-archive/introducing-the-fourth-place -why-third-places-have-fallen-short-on-their-promise.

189. **As Adam Grant puts it:** "The clearest sign of intellectual chemistry isn't agreeing with someone. It's enjoying your disagreements with them. Harmony is the pleasing arrangement of different tones, voices, or instruments, not the combination of identical sounds. Creative tension makes beautiful music." See https://twitter.com/AdamMGrant/status /1375209357865054211.

189. **distributed leadership:** Angela M. Benson and Deborah Blackman, "To Distribute Leadership or Not? A Lesson from the Islands," *Tourism Management* 32, no. 5 (2011): 1141–49.

190. **Encourage autonomy, competence, and relatedness:** Richard M. Ryan and Edward L. Deci, "Self-Determination Theory and the Facilitation

of Intrinsic Motivation, Social Development, and Well-Being," *American Psychologist* 55, no. 1 (2000): 68–78.

CHAPTER 11: LEARNING IN PUBLIC

191. **Galileo could reveal:** Hannah Marcus and Paula Findlen, "Deciphering Galileo: Communication and Secrecy Before and After the Trial," *Renaissance Quarterly* 72, no. 3 (2019): 953–95.

192. **many other scientists used similar devices:** Sascha Friesike et al., "Opening Science: Towards an Agenda of Open Science in Academia and Industry," *Journal of Technology Transfer* 40 (2015): 581–601.

192. **He called this experiment the Polymath Project:** Justin Cranshaw and Aniket Kittur, "The Polymath Project: Lessons from a Successful On-line Collaboration in Mathematics," in *Proceedings of the SIGCHI Conference on Human Factors in Computing Systems*, May 2011, 1865–74, https://www.cs.cmu.edu/~jcransh/papers/cranshaw_kittur.pdf.

192. **"That's a lot of mathematics very quickly":** Michael A. Nielsen, "Reinventing Discovery: The New Era of Networked Science," Carnegie Council for Ethics in International Affairs, transcript and audio, December 7, 2011, https://www.carnegiecouncil.org/media/series/39/20111201-reinventing-discovery-the-new-era-of-networked-science. Michael Nielsen also wrote an eponymous book where he discusses the Polymath Project and open science in general, which I highly recommend reading.

192. **"one of the most exciting six weeks of my mathematical life":** Tim Gowers, "Polymath1 and Open Collaborative Mathematics," *Gowers's Weblog: Mathematics Related Discussions*, March 10, 2009, https://gowers.wordpress.com/2009/03/10/polymath1-and-open-collaborative-mathematics/.

195. **In ancient Greece, learning in public:** Sara Ahbel-Rappe and Rachana Kamtekar, eds., *A Companion to Socrates* (New York: Blackwell Publishing, 2006).

198. **we feel a greater sense of responsibility to follow through:** Philip E. Tetlock, "Accountability Theory: Mixing Properties of Human Agents with Properties of Social Systems," in *Shared Cognition in Organizations: The Management of Knowledge*, ed. Leigh L. Thompson, John M. Levine, and David M. Messick (Mahwah, NJ: Ehrlbaum/Psychology Press, 1999), 117–38.

198. **announcing a goal has the unfortunate effect:** Peter M. Gollwitzer et al., "When Intentions Go Public: Does Social Reality Widen the Intention-Behavior Gap?," *Psychological Science* 20, no. 5 (2009): 612–18.

199. **choosing a familiar platform:** Fred D. Davis, "Perceived Usefulness, Perceived Ease of Use, and User Acceptance of Information Technology," *MIS Quarterly* 13, no. 3 (1989): 319–40.

200. **enhance your belief in your ability to succeed:** Daniel Cervone and Philip K. Peake, "Anchoring, Efficacy, and Action: The Influence of Judgmental Heuristics on Self-Efficacy Judgments and Behavior," *Journal of Personality and Social Psychology* 50, no. 3 (1986): 492–501.

200. **regularly posted sketches online:** Sierra Mon, "Exclusive Interview: Lois van Baarle (Loish)," *ArtStation*, September 20, 2018, https://magazine.artstation.com/2018/09/loish/.

200. **Biochemist Dr. Rhonda Patrick first published:** Tim Ferriss, "A Biochemist Breaks Down Wellness Fads," *Outside*, November 10, 2022, https://www.outsideonline.com/health/wellness/biochemists-advice-wellness/.

200. **Author of fantasy and science fiction Brandon Sanderson began:** Shailee Shah, "9 Unique Ways Authors Engage Readers Through Live Streaming," *BookBub Partners*, February 2, 2023, https://insights.bookbub.com/unique-ways-authors-engage-readers-live-streaming/.

201. **It's a form of iterative learning:** Helen Louise Ackers and James Ackers-Johnson, "Iterative Learning: 'Knowledge for Change'?," in *Mobile Professional Voluntarism and International Development: Killing Me Softly?* (New York: Palgrave Macmillan, 2017), 113–49, https://link.springer.com/book/10.1057/978-1-137-55833-6.

201. **iterating in public creates a culture of learning around yourself:** Mel Green and Jake Young, *Creating Learning Cultures: Assessing the Evidence* (London: Chartered Institute of Personnel and Development, 2020), https://www.cipd.org/globalassets/media/knowledge/knowledge-hub/reports/creating-learning-cultures-1_tcm18-75606.pdf.

202. **Podcast host Steph Smith has a page on her website:** Steph Smith, "Open—Living Life Openly," https://stephsmith.io/open.

202. **vulnerability, which has been found to foster a deeper sense:** Erinn Cunniff Gilson, "Beyond Bounded Selves and Places: The Relational Making of Vulnerability and Security," *Journal of the British Society for Phenomenology* 49, no. 3 (2018): 229–42.

203. **It also builds public trust and engagement:** Nunzio Casalino et al., "Transparency, Openness and Knowledge Sharing for Rebuilding and Strengthening Government Institutions," in WBE 2013 conference, IASTED-ACTA Press Zurich, Innsbruck, Austria, February 2013, https://papers.ssrn.com/sol3/papers.cfm?abstract_id=2553189.

203. **"I found myself having thoughts that I would not have had":** Gowers, "Polymath1 and Open Collaborative Mathematics."

204. **Nomad List brings in about $700,000 in annual revenue:** P. Levels, "How I Got My Startup to #1 on Both Product Hunt and Hacker News by Accident," *levels.io*, August 16, 2014, https://levels.io/product-hunt -hacker-news-number-one/.

206. **Kahl started building a prototype over the weekends:** Arvid Kahl, "From Founding to Exit in Two Years: The FeedbackPanda Story," *The Bootstrapped Founder*, November 9, 2019, https://thebootstrapped founder.com/from-founding-to-exit-in-two-years-the-feedbackpanda -story/.

207. **one of the most common phobias:** Karen Kangas Dwyer and Marlina M. Davidson, "Is Public Speaking Really More Feared Than Death?," *Communication Research Reports* 29, no. 2 (2012): 99–107. Careful! It doesn't mean that people are more scared of public speaking than they are of death, but it is more top-of-mind as a fear.

208. **we fear being judged *poorly*:** Emma C. Winton, David M. Clark, and Robert J. Edelmann, "Social Anxiety, Fear of Negative Evaluation and the Detection of Negative Emotion in Others," *Behaviour Research and Therapy* 33, no. 2 (1995): 193–96.

208. **Psychologists call this *fear of negative evaluation*:** David Watson and Ronald Friend, "Measurement of Social-Evaluative Anxiety," *Journal of Consulting and Clinical Psychology* 33, no. 4 (1969): 448–57.

208. **this fear is not simply psychological, but physical as well:** Graham D. Bodie, "A Racing Heart, Rattling Knees, and Ruminative Thoughts: Defining, Explaining, and Treating Public Speaking Anxiety," *Communication Education* 59, no.1 (2010): 70–105.

208. **the same principle of repeated exposure:** Kainan S. Wang and Mauricio R. Delgado, "The Protective Effects of Perceived Control During Repeated Exposure to Aversive Stimuli," *Frontiers in Neuroscience* 15 (2021): 625816.

209. **By the end of the training:** The training I took is called *UltraSpeaking*, a method created by Michael Gendler and Tristan de Montebello.

209. **talking into a void creates an uncomfortable sense of dissociation:** J. M. P. V. K. Jayasundara et al., "Why Should I Switch On My Camera? Developing the Cognitive Skills of Compassionate Communications for Online Group/Teamwork Management," *Frontiers in Psychology* 14 (2023): 1113098; Alice R. Norton and Maree J. Abbott, "Self-Focused Cognition in Social Anxiety: A Review of the Theoretical and Empirical Literature," *Behaviour Change* 33, no. 1 (2016): 44–64.

212. **reputation relies heavily on public perception:** Claudio Tennie, Uta Frith, and Chris D. Frith, "Reputation Management in the Age of the World-Wide Web," *Trends in Cognitive Sciences* 14, no. 11 (2010): 482–88.

212. **what architects call an intimacy gradient:** The concept of intimacy gradients is particularly important in designing small spaces, which is why it has become an interest of NASA engineers. See Matthew A. Simon and Larry Toups, "Innovation in Deep Space Habitat Interior Design: Lessons Learned from Small Space Design in Terrestrial Architecture," in *AIAA Space 2014 Conference and Exposition*, 4474, https://ntrs.nasa.gov/api/citations/20150001238/downloads/2015 0001238.pdf.

213. **Sharing your work creates an audience effect:** Roser Cañigueral and Antonia F. de C. Hamilton, "Being Watched: Effects of an Audience on Eye Gaze and Prosocial Behaviour," *Acta Psychologica* 195 (2019): 50–63.

213. **The human brain is wired to respond to social feedback:** Patrik Wikman et al., "Brain Responses to Peer Feedback in Social Media Are Modulated by Valence in Late Adolescence," *Frontiers in Behavioral Neuroscience* 16 (2022): 790478.

213. **distorting your priorities:** Gurwinder, "The Perils of Audience Capture: How Influencers Become Brainwashed by Their Audiences," *The Prism* (blog), June 30, 2022, https://www.gurwinder.blog/p/the-perils -of-audience-capture.

213. **Author Stephanie Land faced intense scrutiny:** Ron Lieber, "'Maid' Pulled Stephanie Land out of Poverty. She's Fine Now, Right?," *New York Times*, October 28, 2023, https://www.nytimes.com/2023/10/28 /your-money/maid-stephanie-land-finances.html.

214. **"As a house cleaner":** Lieber, "'Maid' Pulled Stephanie Land out of Poverty."

CHAPTER 12: LIFE BEYOND LEGACY

217. **Giorgio Armani started a career in medicine:** Renata Molho, *Being Armani: A Biography* (Milan: Baldini Castoldi Dalai, 2007).

217. **Harrison Ford was a carpenter:** *Inside the Actors Studio*, season 6, episode 13, "Harrison Ford," August 20, 2000.

217. **Pope Francis II was a bouncer:** Daniel Burke, "Pope: I Was Once a Bar Bouncer," CNN, December 3, 2013.

218. **In 2021, Zapier, a startup worth $5 billion:** Alex Wilhelm, "Zapier Buys No-Code-Focused Makerpad in Its First Acquisition," *TechCrunch*, March 8, 2021.

220. **"ability to transcend personal interests":** Erik H. Erikson, *Childhood and Society* (New York: W. W. Norton, 1993).

221. **wrote investor Patrick O'Shaughnessy:** Patrick O'Shaughnessy (@patrick_oshag), "The most powerful thing I am aware of is to spend your

time doing what you want to do" X (formerly Twitter), November 22, 2023, 9:56 a.m., https://twitter.com/patrick_oshag/status/172734028 6982967711.

221. **"not to instill ambition in others":** David Whyte, "Ambition," in *Consolations: The Solace, Nourishment and Underlying Meaning of Everyday Words* (Many Rivers Press, 2015).

223. **said entrepreneur and investor Sam Altman:** Sam Altman (@sama). "'Give yourself a lot of shots to get lucky' is even better advice than it appears on the surface. Luck isn't an independent variable but increases super-linearly with more surface area—you meet more people, make more connections between new ideas, learn patterns, etc.," X (formerly Twitter), August 27, 2023, 8:30 a.m., https://x.com/sama/status/1695 775873545183584.

223. **"No matter how isolated you are and how lonely you feel":** *C. G. Jung Letters, Volume 2: 1951–1961*, Bollingen Series, ed. Gerhard Adler, trans. Jeffrey Hulen (Princeton, NJ: Princeton University Press, 1976), 595.

224. **In the plant world, lateral roots play a crucial role:** *Encyclopedia of Applied Plant Sciences*, 2nd ed., ed. Brian Thomas, Brian Murray, and Denis J. Murphy, vol. 1 (Amsterdam: Elsevier Academic, 2017), 256–64.

224. **explained sociologist Andrew Abbott:** Andrew Abbott, "Aims of Education—University of Chicago Address 2002," University of Chicago, https://college.uchicago.edu/student-life/aims-education-address -2002-andrew-abbott.

225. **circle of competence:** Warren Buffett, *The Essays of Warren Buffett: Lessons for Investors and Managers,* ed. Lawrence A. Cunningham (Hoboken, NJ: Wiley, 2021).

227. **said author Anna Quindlen:** Anna Quindlen, "1999 Mount Holyoke Commencement Speech," quoted in James Clear (website), https:// jamesclear.com/great-speeches/1999-mount-holyoke-commencement -speech-by-anna-quindlen.

227. **As former magazine editor Farrah Storr puts it:** Lauren Sams, "Is the Personal Brand Dead?," *InStyle Australia*, 2022, https://instyleaustra lia.com.au/death-of-personal-brand/.

227. **co-invented an early version of frequency-hopping spread spectrum:** Tony Rothman, "Random Paths to Frequency Hopping," *American Scientist* 107, no. 1 (2019): 46, https://www.americanscientist.org/arti cle/random-paths-to-frequency-hopping.

227. **Vera Wang's transition in her forties from figure skater:** Edward Barsamian, "Vera on Ice," *New York Times*, December 20, 2011, https:// archive.nytimes.com/tmagazine.blogs.nytimes.com/2011/12/20/vera -on-ice/.

227. **Tim Ferriss, who began his career in data storage:** Stephanie Rosenbloom, "The World According to Tim Ferriss," *New York Times*, March 25, 2011, https://www.nytimes.com/2011/03/27/fashion/27Ferris.html.

228. **The rise of multipotentialites, slashies, and neo-generalists:** Kerry Platman, "'Portfolio Careers' and the Search for Flexibility in Later Life," *Work, Employment and Society* 18, no. 3 (2004): 573–99.

228. **Multihyphenate professionals:** Nikki Shaner-Bradford, "The Rise of the Multi-Hyphenate," *The Outline*, November 25, 2019, https://the outline.com/post/8301/everyone-you-know-is-a-multi-hyphenate.

229. **detailed "postmortems" of their failed ventures:** John H. Mason and Jeffrey S. Hornsby, "Autopsy: Post Mortem Analysis of the Root Causes of 105 Failed Startups," in *United States Association for Small Business and Entrepreneurship Conference Proceedings*, no. 1, 151–58, https://www.proquest.com/openview/7b21d0f8241d1d16269c472f9 f81c613/1?pq-origsite=gscholar&cbl=38818.

229. **Even failure becomes generative:** Maribel Guerrero and Iñaki Peña-Legazkue, "Renascence After Post-Mortem: The Choice of Accelerated Repeat Entrepreneurship," *Small Business Economics* 52 (2019): 47–65.

229. **When Evan Baehr's startup Outbox folded:** Evan Baehr and Will Davis, "Outbox Is Shutting Down—A Note of Gratitude," *Outbox* (blog), January 21, 2014, https://outboxmail.tumblr.com/post/74086768959 /outbox-is-shutting-down-a-note-of-gratitude.

229. **enabled him to maintain the trust of investors:** Blake Bartlett, "Meet the Harvard MBA Who Turned Down Facebook to Found a Startup," *OpenView* (blog), April 15, 2015, https://openviewpartners.com/blog /evan-baehr-able-founder-interview/.

229. **a managing partner at a venture capital fund focused on human flourishing:** Evan Baehr (website), https://www.evanbaehr.com/.

230. **Playfulness fosters creativity:** Charalampos Mainemelis and Sarah Ronson, "Ideas Are Born in Fields of Play: Towards a Theory of Play and Creativity in Organizational Settings," *Research in Organizational Behavior* 27 (2006): 81–131.

231. **"It is much easier to be fired":** Rory Sutherland, *Alchemy: The Dark Art and Curious Science of Creating Magic in Brands, Business, and Life* (New York: Mariner, 2019).

231. **White started baking cakes:** Hilarey Wojtowicz, "This Instagram Star's Sweet Side Hustle Became an Even Tastier Full-Time Gig," *Swirled*, March 20, 2019, https://swirled.com/chelsweets-side-hustle.

231. **entrepreneur Josh Pigford, who has launched dozens of ventures:** *Trouble Makers*, podcast, season 1, episode 3, "Open Startups with Josh Pigford," *Maker Mag*, April 29, 2019.

232. **Injecting playfulness into your work:** Yuri S. Scharp et al., "Daily Playful Work Design: A Trait Activation Perspective," *Journal of Research in Personality* 82 (2019): 103850.

232. **exploring unobvious paths and reframing problems:** Or, as Roger Skaer elegantly puts it: "In order to find out anything, an appropriate amount of fucking around will be required." Twitter (now X), October 28, 2022, 11:16 a.m., https://twitter.com/rogerskaer/status/15860140 28358619136.

233. **John Keats famously wrote:** John Keats, *The Poems of John Keats*, ed. Ernest De Sélincourt (New York: Dodd, Mead, 1905), 53.

INDEX

ABOUT THE AUTHOR

Anne-Laure Le Cunff is an award-winning neuroscientist, entrepreneur, and writer. Her research focuses on the neuro-developmental basis of lifelong learning and curiosity. She is the founder of Ness Labs and author of its widely read news-letter, a researcher at the ADHD Research Lab, and an advi-sor for the Applied Neuroscience Association. She holds a PhD in psychology and neuroscience from King's College London and teaches the course Neuroscience in the Digital World at the Institute of Psychiatry, Psychology & Neurosci-ence. She previously worked at Google as a global lead on digital health projects. She lives in London.